The Challenge of Antarctica

Eleanor Honnywill

The Challenge of Antarctica

with a Foreword by Sir Vivian Fuchs

Anthony Nelson

This new edition published 1984 by Anthony Nelson
PO Box 9, Oswestry, Shropshire SY11 1BY, England
First published in 1969 by Methuen & Company Limited,
London EC4

ISBN 0 904614093

Designed by Alan Bartram

Phototypeset and printed by BAS Printers Limited,
Over Wallop, Hampshire

Contents

List of maps

List of illustrations

Author's note and Acknowledgments

In this revised and expanded version of a book first published in 1969 emphasis has been laid on the early expeditions, of which accounts are not easily accessible. I am very conscious of the many gaps left in a necessarily abbreviated story of Antarctic discovery, but I hope that readers may be stimulated to look at some of the original accounts of expeditions which have been omitted. A chronological list of the main ones is given on page 122.

I acknowledge with gratitude the generous help given me by the late Sir Raymond Priestley and by Sir Vivian Fuchs in the preparation of the manuscript.

I would also like to thank Miss G. E. Todd of the British Antarctic Survey for all her help and encouragement.

Author and publishers gratefully acknowledge permission to reproduce illustrations from the following:

The Australian Information Service, London 17, 22, 33, 34, 36
Royal Geographical Society 1, 10, 13, 14, 15, 16, 27
Scott Polar Research Institute 2, 3, 4, 5, 12, 20
British Antarctic Survey, 21, 31, 35
Trans-Antarctic Expedition Committee 23, 24, 25, 26, 30
BBC Hulton Picture Library 6, 7
The British Library 11
New Zealand High Commission, London 8, 9, 18
United States Navy 28, 32
United States Information Service 19
Illustrated Newspapers Ltd 29
Maps by Edgar Holloway

For
Annabelle and Richard Honnywill
and
Emma and Harriet Butler

Foreword by Sir Vivian Fuchs

I am delighted that *The Challenge of Antarctica* is republished in an updated form. When I wrote a Foreword to the first edition, I spoke of a community of nations working under a Treaty which has dedicated the continent to science. This remains true today, but a new factor – the potential resources of Antarctica – may influence the signatories when the time comes to review the Treaty in 1991.

The early story of exploration and discovery remains the same. It is a tale of imagination and endeavour which must surely stir everyone in whom there is a spark of adventure. For all the modern equipment and techniques, Nature continues to challenge the intruder. But just as scientific investigation replaced geographical discovery, so now science is opening the way for the beginning of exploitation. For this, entirely new advances will be necessary, whether it be to recover minerals from beneath thousands of feet of ice, or oil from the deep continental shelf.

Yet it should not be forgotten that such endeavours, like the scientific studies of today, are all founded on the past spirit and daring of hardy men, who first learnt how to survive and work in an unknown and cruelly hostile environment.

In this book the great feats of the past are told in a brief but lively style, which must surely stimulate the young and provide a sense of wonder to their elders.

London 1983

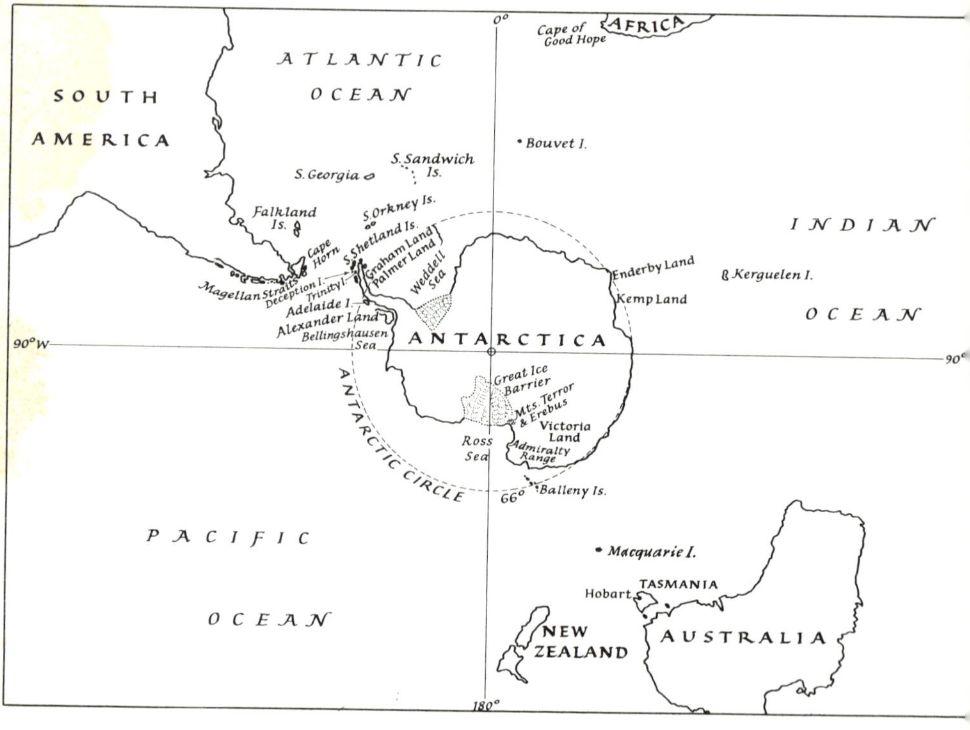

Map 1. Antarctica and the southern continents

I

The Search for a South Land

Antarctica is the largest, highest, coldest and cruellest desert in the world. Unlike the Arctic, it is a huge landmass, as big as Europe and Australia together, with the Atlantic, Pacific and Indian Oceans beating against its coastline. The continent is almost entirely covered by a great ice sheet, through which rise long mountain ranges whose peaks reach 16,000 feet. The greatest thickness of ice so far measured is over 14,000 feet.

Almost in the middle of the high polar plateau lies the South Pole. There the average temperature is $-60°$F, which is ninety-two degrees of frost. The lowest temperature so far recorded in Antarctica is $-124°$F. More than 90 per cent of the ice in the whole world is locked up here, and if it suddenly melted, sea level all over the world would rise 180 feet, drowning our coastal towns. All this ice is slowly moving downhill. When it reaches the coast it breaks off to form huge flat-topped 'tabular' icebergs, sometimes as much as 50 or 100 miles in length, which gradually disintegrate as they float out into the southern oceans.

During summer the sun never sets, but in winter it never rises and the seas around Antarctica freeze, forming great belts of pack ice, in places 1000 miles wide. Glistening icebergs are gripped fast in the pack, rising out of the frozen sea to guard the shores of this isolated continent, until they are released by the summer thaw.

Glaciers are the rivers of Antarctica. There are no trees, no flowers, no soil, no land animals, no germs and no inhabitants. Icy winds gusting to 100 knots constantly scour the snow surface, filling the air with blinding drift. But in good weather the atmosphere is so clear that mountain ranges can be seen from 150 miles away, while the sound of voices or the howling of huskies can carry for long distances. All who have been there find it difficult to describe the grandeur and majesty of this harsh land of brilliant colours. It is perhaps the most beautiful and terrifying place in the world.

The idea of an Antarctic region was conceived by the ancient Greeks some three thousand years before the continent we know today was finally discovered. As they studied the stars wheeling round the heavens, they gave names to the brightest groups. The most conspicuous of the constellations, one which never set, they called *Arctos* – the Bear. The point round which it seemed constantly to revolve was called the Arctic Pole.

Whilst believing that the world was a flat disc, they could think of a similar fixed point, or *Antarctic* Pole, under the Earth. This they imagined as a region of terror where it was forever dark and which, over a thousand years later, the early Christians thought of as Hell. Later Greek philosophers decided that the most perfect form in art is a sphere. Since man was considered the perfect creation, they argued that the world on which he lived must be spherical. Three hundred years before Christ, Aristotle demonstrated that the Earth is round because no other shape could throw a circular shadow on to the moon during an eclipse. So the Greeks came to accept the idea of a southern zone of extreme cold, similar to the region that they knew lay to the north of them. Here lay the *Terra Incognita* shown on all the old maps, a great unknown 'South Land' which could never be reached.

With the coming of Christianity all this changed. It was then thought impossible that anyone could cross the burning gulf of the Equator. The early Christian Fathers would not admit the possibility of an inhabited region on the other side of the globe, for this implied a whole region of the Earth to which the Gospel could not be carried. They denounced the enlightened Greek theories as heresy, and as a result there was a gap in our knowledge of the world for the next 1400 years.

From time to time the old ideas were revived. Voyages of discovery at last forced the Church to admit that the Earth must be a globe and the Pope himself began to encourage maritime exploration. He divided the world in half along the forty-sixth meridian, and decreed that the Portuguese should explore the regions to the east while the Spanish were confined to the west.

A wealth of discovery took place throughout the sixteenth and seventeenth centuries, by such famous explorers as Diaz, Magellan who circumnavigated the southern hemisphere, Drake, Tasman and many more. But the chronometer was not invented until the middle of the eighteenth century and it was impossible to make accurate charts. In addition, the early buccaneers, who were chiefly seeking trade for their countries, were often unwilling to say exactly where they had seen land, with the result that a great deal of confused and inaccurate information was added to the maps of the southern oceans. The Solomon Islands, the New Hebrides, New Guinea, Tasmania and parts of New Zealand were each in turn thought to be the South Land.

Ships rounding Cape Horn were often driven south off their course and found themselves in icy seas, but it was a Frenchman, Jean Bouvet de Lozier, who first made a determined effort to find the southern continent. His voyage in 1739 resulted in the discovery of the sub-Antarctic Iles Bouvet. His were the first descriptions of tabular icebergs, and his reports of having seen penguins and seals indicated the proximity of land.

1. The world according to Ptolemy, 1540

In 1756 a Spanish ship, the *Leon*, sailed past mountainous land covered in snow. This was later found by Captain Cook who named it the Isle of Georgia. Sixteen years later Yves Joseph de Kerguelen-Tremarec sailed from Mauritius in search of a southern continent. He discovered only a very inhospitable island which, in disgust, he called the Isle of Desolation; later it was renamed in his honour as Kerguelen Island.

So the voyages multiplied, in conditions of terrible hardship. The crew's quarters were unbelievably cramped. Always short of water, their diet consisted mainly of salt beef or pork, which gradually rotted as a voyage lengthened, and black bread which soon went mouldy and became infested with cockroaches.

In the story of the discovery of the South Land, the most important figure of all is Captain James Cook. The son of a Yorkshire farm labourer, he ran away to sea as a boy, joined a coal-ship and worked his way up to mate. He then joined the Navy, and in 1768 he was given command of a small scientific expedition to the southern hemisphere. In the course of this voyage he circumnavigated New Zealand, and thus proved conclusively that it did not form part of a southern continent.

2. HMS Resolution *watering ship from an iceberg*

Four years later the Admiralty sent out a new expedition, again under Cook's command, charged with discovering and charting the South Land, or disproving the theory once and for all. The *Resolution* (462 tons) and the *Adventure* (336 tons) were provisioned for two years. Cook himself made elaborate arrangements for fresh food, and was the first captain to insist on a measure of hygiene in the crew's quarters.

The ships sailed from Plymouth in July 1772 and on 10 December, south of the African continent, they met the first icebergs. A fierce storm was raging, the sea was high and there was thick fog. Large fields of pack ice constantly blocked the way, but Cook persisted on a southerly course whenever possible, and on 17 January 1773 the Antarctic Circle was crossed for the first time. This is the parallel of 66°30′S, on which for one 24-hour period in each year the sun remains above the horizon in summer and is hidden in winter. Further south the time increases, until at the South Pole itself there are six months of constant summer sunlight, followed by six months of total darkness. The short southern summer, when sea ice thaws, lasts from about mid-November until the end of March. So Cook was soon forced to sail north again to winter in New Zealand.

The following season the *Resolution* again set out for the South Land, this time crossing the Antarctic Circle due south of New Zealand. From here Cook tried to keep an easterly course within the Circle, always sailing as far south as the ice fields permitted, and always searching for signs of land. His path was continually blocked by immense bergs, and high seas battered his little ship unmercifully. This time she struggled through to reach latitude 70°10′S, longitude 106°54′W, the most southerly point to which a ship had ever penetrated. Cook wrote in his diary:

> I will not say that it was impossible anywhere to get farther to the south, but attempting it would have been a dangerous and rash enterprise, and which I believe no man, in my opinion, would have thought of. It was, indeed, my opinion . . . that this ice extended quite to the Pole.

Thankfully they turned back for the winter.

On 10 November 1774, the *Resolution* set sail for the third time. On 14 January 1775, land was sighted. Three landings were made at different points, the Union Jack was hoisted and Cook took possession of the Isle of Georgia 'in His Majesty's name'. Then he entered the ice in the area now known as the Weddell Sea, but here the pack was so thick that he was forced to the north-east. As a result, he discovered the South Sandwich Islands.

By the end of his third season, Cook had circled the Earth as far south as it was possible to sail a ship, and the great ice fields which he had seen convinced him that a frigid continent must exist within the Antarctic Circle. His greatest contribution to exploration was not what he discovered, but rather what he proved did *not* exist. His voyages, and his accurate navigation, swept away all the errors on the existing maps of the southern oceans, leaving them almost completely empty – ready for the true southern continent, the South Land itself, to be unveiled.

2
The Age of the Sealers

Captain Cook's reports had told of large colonies of fur seals hauled out on the beaches of the Isle of Georgia (now known as South Georgia). At the end of the eighteenth century, when mineral oils were unknown, whale oil and seal blubber were in great demand for lighting, and were also used for preserving ships' ropes, sails and timbers. The sudden advent of the industrial revolution created an immediate demand for oil to lubricate the new machine parts. Also about this time, seal skins began to be fashionable for women's coats. Large fleets of whalers and sealers brought back the harvest of the northern seas, but in the Arctic, stocks were beginning to diminish.

Cook's discoveries alerted the merchants of England and America. The sealing fleets made for the beaches of South Georgia with all speed. There followed one of the most terrible examples of Man's depredation of animal life, which within fifty years led almost to the extermination of an entire species.

The sealers suffered great hardship in following their brutal trade. They sailed uncharted, ice-filled seas, and worked ashore caked in grease and often up to their thighs in blood. But the crews were paid in proportion to the cargoes

3. *Sealing on pack ice*

they brought home and soon became indifferent to the cruelty they inflicted. In 1778 English sealers alone took from the Isle of Georgia and the Magellan Straits 40,000 seal skins and 2800 tons of sea elephant oil, the latter valued at £40,000.

It is not certain when the first American sealers arrived, but by 1825 they were carrying large cargoes of skins from South Georgia to China, where they fetched $5 apiece. The skippers often saw huge ice formations which might have been land, but always it was impossible to work through the heavy belts of pack ice to investigate more closely. For the first forty years after Cook's last voyage we know little of what was really seen and charted.

In February 1819 an English captain, William Smith, in the brig *Williams*, discovered the South Shetland Islands. Here he found seals in abundance. The islands soon became the centre of profitable trade, until within ten years the fur seals were exterminated. However, as a result of his discovery, a naval expedition under the command of Edward Bransfield was sent on a voyage of exploration. His orders were to survey the coastline of the South Shetlands, to take soundings, and to report on the natural resources and the character and customs of the inhabitants.

Having carried out his instructions, and finding the islands uninhabited, Bransfield sailed yet further south. On 30 January 1820 his ship was in thick fog, surrounded by reefs and icebergs. Then the haze cleared, and all of a sudden they saw land to the south-west.

In fact it was Trinity Island, but behind it, hidden by the fog and separated only by a narrow strait, lay mountains extending to the south. When the fog lifted completely the coastline appeared, and two high peaks were sighted. Antarctica – the seventh continent – had been found at last!

American sealing fleets sent south by the merchants of Stonington, Connecticut, were also active in the South Shetlands area. The following season, in November 1820, five vessels under the command of Captain Benjamin Pendleton arrived, to be joined later by a fleet of other ships. Whilst searching for new grounds, the Stonington flotilla came to Deception Island, where there was a natural harbour formed by the sea breaching and filling the crater of an extinct volcano, through a narrow break in its side. A landing was made and Captain Pendleton climbed a high ridge, from where he thought he sighted land to the south. Nathanial Palmer, in command of a 45-ton sloop called *Hero*, was sent to investigate. Thus it was that, knowing nothing of Bransfield's previous voyage, Palmer in turn discovered the coastline of the southern continent.

Both nations claimed the credit for the first sighting, and bitter arguments later developed as armchair geographers in both countries sought to discredit the claims of two honest men.

4. Jane *and* Beaufoy *in the Weddell Sea*

During the next twenty years many famous navigators, some naval captains but most of them sealing skippers, contributed to the charting of the new continent. One of these was a Russian, Thaddeus von Bellingshausen, whose painstaking and accurate surveys in the *Vostok* and the *Mirny* added a great deal to the maps of the time. Another was the Englishman James Weddell, who spent several years sealing in the South Shetlands.

Cruising south in 1821 in the *Jane*, Weddell discovered the South Orkney Islands. Two years later, accompanied by the *Beaufoy*, he sailed due south of these islands, determined to find out where the coastline of the continent itself began. The ships penetrated to 74°15′S, far beyond the latitude reached by Cook some fifty years before, but the onset of winter forced them to turn back before land was sighted. Nonetheless, Weddell's achievement is astonishing, for we now know that along this part of the Antarctic coast the pack ice is normally 1000 miles wide and most of it remains frozen throughout the summer. The year 1823 must have been an exceptionally 'open' season: now named the Weddell Sea, this is the most dreaded stretch of water around the continent.

The English trading company of Enderby Brothers played a major part in exploration at this time. Charles Enderby encouraged his captains to 'pursue discovery with a view to the advancement of knowledge', and Kemp Land and the Balleny Islands were discoverd by, and named after two of his skippers. Best known among them is John Biscoe, a retired master, Royal Navy, who commanded the schooner *Tula*. In 1830, accompanied by the small cutter *Lively*, he sailed to the South Sandwich Islands hoping to find seals, but it was impossible to land on the steep volcanic shores. Biscoe then set a southerly course which took the ships into dense pack ice. In this they 'were utterly prevented from steering on any one course for more than a few minutes at a time', but despite the difficulties they found Enderby Land, which Biscoe named in honour of his owners.

Soon after this their troubles began, for a great storm arose and the *Tula* was driven before the wind for 120 miles before the weather moderated and the captain regained control. The crew were decimated by scurvy, the carpenter died, and eventually the ship was being worked by the captain, two mates, one man and a boy. They turned north and were thankful to reach Tasmania in May.

Meanwhile the *Lively* had continued her cruise alone, only turning back when deaths had reduced her company to three. Suffering terrible hardships they sailed her back to Tasmania, and it says much for the courage and endurance of the early seamen that, by the following season, both ships had fresh crews and were headed south once more.

During his second voyage Biscoe discovered Adelaide Island, and on 19 February 1832 he was the first man to land on the mainland itself. He named it Graham Land, after the First Lord of the Admiralty.

The argument about its first discovery was still raging, and for more than a century all American maps showed this feature as Palmer Land. It was not until 1964 that a more co-operative spirit prevailed on both sides, and it was agreed that the northern half of the peninsula would be known as Graham Land, and the southern half as Palmer Land. The whole feature was given the name Antarctic Peninsula.

3
Beginnings of Scientific Exploration

During the first half of the nineteenth century, many learned societies were founded, and scientists all over Europe were particularly interested in the study of the Earth's magnetic fields. The North and South Poles represent the two ends of an imaginary axle about which the world revolves. But many voyages to the polar regions had demonstrated that while over the greater part of the Earth the needle of a magnetic compass points north-south, in high latitudes this is not so. Here the needle is drawn not to the true pole, but to a strong magnetic field, the centre of which is called the Magnetic Pole.

The position of the North Magnetic Pole had already been determined by a naval expedition which had spent four years in the Arctic, and among its members was James Clark Ross. He was kindly, generous, and reputed to be the handsomest man in the Navy. In 1838 the Admiralty decided to fit out an expedition to make magnetic surveys in the southern hemisphere, and attempt to fix the position of the South Magnetic Pole. Captain Ross was given command of two stoutly built ships, the *Erebus* and *Terror*. Britain was then the greatest maritime power in the world, and this was the best equipped expedition which had ever been sent to the Antarctic. For the first time the ships were strong enough to challenge the great belt of pack ice which had blocked the passage of all vessels since the days of Captain Cook.

Sailing from Tasmania, Ross reached the edge of the pack in January 1841 and steered straight into it, charging the floes to break them up. In only four days the ships were worked through the ice. Suddenly they were sailing in open water, and on the verge of the most spectacular new discovery. To their utter amazement the men saw before them huge ice cliffs rising up to 200 feet above the sea, while in the distance great mountain peaks extended out of sight.

Ross named the great landmass which faced them Victoria Land, after the Queen, and the mountains, the Admiralty Range. Cruising westward along the magnificent coastline, they found a barrier of ice which extended to the horizon and barred the way south. This they called the Great Ice Barrier (now the Ross Ice Shelf). Two volcanoes, from one of which white plumes of smoke curled gently up into the blue sky, were named Mount Erebus and Mount Terror. But magnetic observations showed that the South Magnetic Pole lay some 500 miles inland, and the expedition was not equipped to reach it.

5. HMS Erebus *and* HMS Terror *'. . . in an ocean of rolling fragments of ice . . .'*

Nevertheless, much scientific work was carried out before winter set in. The following season Ross sailed south once again. This time there was no easy passage through the pack. Progress was exasperatingly slow and in January, while the ships sailed slowly through the fog, a gale sprang up. Ross described their struggle:

> Soon after midnight our ships were involved in an ocean of rolling fragments of ice, hard as floating rocks of granite, which were dashed against them by the waves with so much violence that their masts quivered as if they would fall at every successive blow; and the destruction of the ships seemed inevitable from the tremendous shocks they received. By backing and filling the sails we endeavoured to avoid collision with the larger masses, but this was not always possible; in the early part of the storm the rudder of the *Erebus* was so much damaged as to be no longer of any use; and about the same time I was informed by signal that the *Terror's* was completely destroyed, and nearly torn away from the stern-post.

When the storm abated they continued their magnetic work, fighting their way through 800 miles of pack ice, which this season extended right up to the edge of the Great Ice Barrier. It was so cold that the decks and the rigging were covered in frozen spray. A small fish dashed against the bows of the *Terror* was frozen to the ship's side and quickly became a block of ice. It was carefully hacked out for the scientists, but unfortunately the ship's cat found it first.

By 6 March 1842, the ships had been battling with ice for sixty-four days. Winter was coming, and Ross set course for the Falkland Islands. For weeks they had sailed as close as possible to the coast, charting the direction in which the Barrier trended, taking soundings and continuing the magnetic surveys. Now as they sailed in a calm sea with a clear sky, the wind suddenly rose and heavy snow showers reduced visibility. Ice floes appeared all round them, a large berg lay dead ahead:

> . . . just at this moment the *Terror* was observed running down upon us . . . and as it was impossible for her to clear both the berg and the *Erebus*, collision was inevitable.

As she struck, the men were thrown off their feet, the ships hung together entangled by their rigging 'dashing against each other with fearful violence'. Eventually the *Terror* was washed free and managed to clear the end of the berg against which they were driven. The *Erebus* was so badly damaged that Ross had no alternative but to try and sail her out of her predicament stern first by 'backing her main yard'. The gale was still at its height:

> . . . amidst the roar of the wind and sea it was difficult both to hear and to execute the orders that were given, so that it was three quarters of an hour before we could get the yards braced bye and the main tack hauled on board sharp aback – an expedient that perhaps had never been resorted to by seamen in such weather; but it had the desired effect; the ship gathered sternway, plunging her stern into the sea, washing away the gig and quarter boats, and with her lower yardarms scraping the rugged face of the berg, we in a few minutes reached its western termination . . .

For four seasons Ross pursued his discoveries along the coast of Antarctica, everywhere correcting or adding to the existing charts. His work was meticulous and accurate, and his voyages were as geographically important as those of Captain Cook. The Ross Sea was fittingly named in his honour.

The first men ever to winter within the Antarctic Circle did so involuntarily, for their ship was beset in the ice. The International Geographical Congress of 1895 had passed a resolution declaring that 'the exploration of the Antarctic Regions is the greatest piece of geographical exploration still to be undertaken'. This acted as a spur, and during the next ten years seven major expeditions were organised. The first was led by Lieutenant Adrien de Gerlache, a Belgian naval officer, while the First Mate was a Norwegian called Roald Amundsen. Their ship was the *Belgica* (250 tons).

The expedition sailed from Ostend in 1897, reaching the South Shetland Islands in January the following year. Some 200 miles of the west coast of Graham Land were charted, and many landings were made to collect geological and biological specimens. Where they found exposed rock they sometimes also found mosses and lichens. But while de Gerlache was sympathetic to the demands of science, the scientists were not encouraged to linger over their work. The geologist gives a delightful account of one such landing when the leader himself rowed them ashore.

> A few strokes of the oars brought us to the beach amid cries of 'Hurry up, Arctowski!' I gave a hammer to Tellefsen with orders to chip here and there down by the shore, while I hurriedly climbed the moraine, picking up specimens as I ran, took the direction with my compass, glanced to the left and right, and hurried down again full speed to get a look at the rock *in situ*. Meanwhile, Cook had taken a photograph of the place from the ship—and that is the way geological surveys have to be carried out in the Antarctic!

It was a bad ice season. When the *Belgica* reached the latitude of Alexander Land she found the edge of the pack. During a gale, this broke up into small fields of hummocky ice floes separated by narrow leads. Against the advice of his companions de Gerlache insisted on sailing up a lead, hoping to get further south. With a sudden change of wind the pack closed in behind him – the ship was beset. The sun disappeared and winter came. For thirteen months the *Belgica* was held relentlessly in an icy grip, drifting helplessly to and fro as the winds and currents carried the floe which imprisoned her.

The men were physically and psychologically quite unprepared for such a severe experience. They suffered from lack of the right kind of food, and there was insufficient heavy clothing. Fierce storms blew round them and cracked the ice. The groaning and crashing noises it made in the endless night were a horror to which they never became accustomed. One of the men died of his privations; everyone was affected to some degree, both in mind and body. To counter their lethargy they walked round and round the ship, and this icy path soon became known as 'madhouse promenade'.

Sometimes the ice was lit by a cold, brilliant moon, sometimes by magical curtains of weird lights which flickered in the night sky – the *aurora australis* or Southern Lights, which appear when particles emitted by the invisible sun interact with the denser layers of the Earth's atmosphere.

Yet despite their ordeals the expedition was remarkable for the amount of scientific work which was accomplished. Meteorological observations were maintained. Although the ice thickened to 10 feet, holes were cut through which they fished for plankton. Whenever the sounding line found sea bottom, they dredged up samples for examination. Continuous records were kept of the depths and temperature of the sea under the ice, and of the currents affecting the floe.

On 22 July the sun returned and their spirits revived. As the seals and penguins came back, hunting parties were organised, and with a more varied diet their health improved. Unfortunately it was an unusually cold summer and the pack remained solid around them. The floe holding the ship fast remained some 10 feet thick and 4 miles in diameter. Unless it broke up they would remain imprisoned for another winter.

By January they were desperate, and began trying to blast a narrow lane to the edge of the floe, just wide enough for the passage of the ship. The work was so hard that they found themselves eating seven meals a day. On the 14th the wind at last veered to help them, and the ship broke loose. But it was still another month before she could be worked painfully back to the open sea and safety.

So ended a century during which human endeavour had opened the door to the last continent. The existence of a South Land had been proved. Commerce following upon discovery had almost exterminated the fur seals, and had in turn been succeeded by the first scientific expeditions. The stage was set for the 'heroic age' of exploration, which was to be overtaken by political discord.

4
Towards the Pole

The beginning of the twentieth century saw the era we now speak of as the heroic age of polar exploration. At that time no one knew how to live or travel efficiently in the cruellest environment in the world. No one knew what kinds of food, and in what quantities, are essential to sustain a man doing hard physical work in bitter cold. Each expedition was an experiment. Each in turn pioneered different types of warm clothing, sledging rations, and the means and techniques of travel. No one knew what sort of conditions to expect in the interior of the great, white, virgin desert. Of those who went to find out, perhaps few ever dreamt they could be as bad as they were.

Here it is impossible to mention the extraordinary achievements of all the men who contributed so much to our present knowledge, but the full stories can be found in their own modest accounts of their adventures.

Two of the greatest leaders among them were Captain Robert Falcon Scott and Sir Ernest Shackleton.

The British National Antarctic Expedition, 1901–1904

In response to the spirit of scientific exploration in Antarctica, a British expedition was organised and Captain Scott, Royal Navy was chosen to command it. He was a man of many contradictions. As a child Scott was frail, moody, quick-tempered and lazy. He grew into a highly intelligent young man, with a great interest in science but over-sensitive, shy and withdrawn. The sight of blood made him feel sick. In the Antarctic the necessity to kill and gut seals was a terrible ordeal, but in all things Scott disciplined his own nature until, by sheer strength of character, he developed a driving force which became the inspiration of his companions. He turned out to be the hardest sledger of them all, forcing himself to keep going in impossible conditions far longer than a stronger man might have attempted. He welded together a team of men who were proud to follow him, but his greatest victory was over himself.

His ship, the *Discovery*, was built in Dundee. She was of solid oak, and carried powerful auxiliary engines capable of battling with ice. Fitted out for oceanographic work, an area of her hull was kept free of all metal so that accurate magnetic observations could be made.

The expedition sailed from Cowes on 6 August 1901, with a ship's company

6. '. . . a balloon was set up on the ice'

of 50 men and 19 Greenland huskies. Young Lieutenant Ernest Shackleton was one of the deck officers. The surgeon and zoologist was Dr Edward Wilson, a deeply religious man, full of humour and great tact, to whom everyone turned for advice. He was also a talented artist. In many hundreds of water colours he caught the grandeur and beauty of the unknown continent, and with painstaking accuracy he illustrated the scientific work of the expedition.

On her arrival in Antarctica, it took less than a week for the *Discovery* to forge her way through the pack ice into the open waters of the Ross Sea. Soon the white plume of Mount Erebus could be seen. They cruised southwards along the Victoria Land coast and then eastward along the Great Ice Barrier, charting some 1200 miles of coastline, and at its eastern extremity new land was discovered. This they named King Edward VII Land, and here the ship turned back. Returning along the Barrier they made a landing, and a hydrogen balloon was set up on the ice, anchored by wire ropes. When this was inflated Scott was the first man to ascend in the basket. It rose to over 600 feet and he was able to see a long distance inland. Far away to

7. Man-hauling on the Barrier

the south the great Barrier seemed to end, and the land rose up abruptly as great mountain chains split by glaciers. The Pole itself must lie on an immense high plateau which was faintly visible behind them.

Returning to McMurdo Sound, the *Discovery* was anchored in a sheltered harbour on the south side of Ross Island. Soon new younger ice formed around her until she was safely frozen in for the winter. The island was separated from the mainland by fast sea ice. In case a storm should break this up and prevent sledging parties getting back to the ship, a small hut was built on the mainland to provide shelter. This tongue of land was named Hut Point.

On 23 April the sun disappeared for four months, and a busy winter routine was established. Magnetic work went on in a small hut built near the ship. A tide gauge placed on the ice recorded the rise and fall of the floating Barrier. Holes were bored in the sea ice through which the biologist worked a dredge and lowered his fish traps. A meteorological screen filled with recording instruments was erected a few hundred yards from the ship and these were read at four-hourly intervals day and night.

When spring came and the light returned, sledging parties set out to explore the continent. The most important of these journeys was made by Scott, Wilson and Shackleton in an attempt to find a route to the South Pole. On 2 November they started across the Barrier ice, using all the dogs harnessed in three teams.

Since the length of a journey depended entirely on the amount of food and fuel which could be carried, the daily sledging ration was very meagre. Basically it consisted of pemmican (a concentrate consisting of fat emulsified with beef fibrin, which, when boiled up with snow became a thick stew or 'hoosh'), sledging biscuit, butter, sugar and small quantities of tea or cocoa. The daily allowance of pemmican per man was $7\frac{1}{2}$ oz; it is now known that at least 1 lb per day is necessary for hard sledging. Depots were laid as they travelled, to be picked up on the return journey.

Biting winds blew in their faces, and the Barrier surface was so rough that the dogs could not pull the weights. They were soon forced to 'relay'; this meant carrying half the load forward at a time, setting it down and returning for the remainder. Sometimes they advanced only 4 miles in a day, though in fact they had travelled 12 miles. It was heartbreaking work, and the men became ravenously hungry. Shackleton wrote in his diary:

> We always dream of something to eat when asleep. My general dream is that fine, three-cornered tarts are flying past me upstairs, but I never seem able to stop them.

The surface grew softer and the struggle to move forward harder. One day they advanced only 2 miles in ten hours. By the end of November the dogs began to weaken and die. Their ration of dried fish was also inadequate for the work they were asked to do. But the party held on grimly, the men pulling their hearts out with the teams. On Christmas Day Shackleton was cook, and in the cocoa he prepared for supper he boiled up three tiny squares of plum pudding:

> It only weighed 6 oz, and I had it stowed away in my socks (clean ones) in my sleeping bag . . . It was a glorious surprise to them when I produced it. They immediately got out our emergency allowance of brandy so as to set it on fire in proper style; but when the brandy was uncorked it was found to be black from corrosion . . . and had to be thrown away.

The journey continued until the last day of the year. The Barrier stretched far into the distance to the east, but to the west they could see chain after chain of mountain ranges barring the way to the south. Cliffs rose 1800 feet sheer above the Barrier, and there seemed to be no way through to the high polar plateau behind, which was their goal. The great panorama was magnificent, and at the end of each day's march Wilson sat outside the tent faithfully sketching, while the others plotted their position on the map they were compiling. Determined to get the colours true, Wilson took off his goggles and suffered an acute attack of snow-blindness. For some days afterwards he had to march blindfolded and in great pain.

By the time the party reached latitude 82°15′S all three of them were showing signs of scurvy. They turned for home with just enough food for two weeks. The distance back to the first depot required an average daily march of 7 miles, and it was now a terrible struggle to keep it up. The weakest dogs were killed to feed the remainder. When they reached the depot Shackleton was so ill that he could no longer pull in harness, nor help with the heavy camp work. Only his indomitable will kept him on his feet at all, and his two companions looked after him as best they could. For three more weeks he struggled painfully along beside the sledge. On 3 February 1903, after ninety-four days on the Barrier, the three sick men arrived wearily back at the ship.

The Admiralty had sent out the *Morning* to make sure that the expedition was not in difficulties. When she returned to New Zealand at the end of the season, Shackleton was invalided home on doctor's orders.

The following spring Scott with two seamen, Petty Officer Edgar Evans and Chief Stoker William Lashly, made a long man-hauling journey to the mountains which lay to the west. Ascending the Ferrar Glacier they reached the polar plateau, here 8900 feet high. This was another great feat of endurance, and in relating their adventures Scott paid high tribute to the quality of his companions.

The scientific work of the *Discovery* expedition is recognised as Scott's greatest achievement. Apart from all the biological work done from the ship, his sledging parties covered 3000 miles and discovered 1050 miles of new land or ice shelf. They fixed the height and position of over 200 mountain peaks and found many new glaciers. The Great Ice Barrier was estimated to vary in thickness from 70 to 700 feet above the sea, the submerged part being four times greater, and they found it was moving seaward at the rate of 492 yards each year. By this calculation the ice from a glacier starting in the high snow fields of the plateau and descending to the barrier in the area reached by Scott on the first journey, would take more than 1000 years to arrive at the sea. Sir James Ross had discovered the Great Ice Barrier, but Scott was the first man to explore it. Deservedly he returned home to a hero's welcome – and quite determined one day to go back.

Shackleton's First Expedition, 1907–1909

It was Shackleton who found a route to the Pole. Ernest Shackleton was a large, genial Irishman of Quaker descent. He had a passion for poetry, a tremendously forceful personality, and the ability to inspire those around him with his own optimism and immense powers of endurance. Above all he understood how to manage men, and how to get the last ounce out of them. In a bad situation his companions always had implicit trust in the Boss.

It was the bitterest disappointment of Shackleton's life to be invalided home from the *Discovery*, and his busy mind was soon full of plans for his own expedition. By 1907 he had raised sufficient money to buy the *Nimrod*, a 200-ton sealing schooner. When he announced his plans, he was able to pick his team from thousands of eager young men who volunteered for the new venture.

Shackleton had realised that the key to successful polar travel was the means of transport. On Scott's expedition the dogs had not done well, so Shackleton decided to take ten Manchurian ponies, and – a motor car (*see fig.* 29)! The expedition sailed on 7 August 1907, reaching New Zealand in three and a half months. From there the *Nimrod* was towed to the Antarctic Circle to conserve fuel. Shackleton established his winter quarters at Cape Royds on Ross Island, immediately under the slopes of Mount Erebus. A hut was built, and the ship returned to New Zealand, leaving behind fifteen men.

Three main journeys were made during this expedition. Before winter set in, Professor Edgeworth David, who had joined the party in Australia, led a party of six men up Mount Erebus. It took six days to reach the summit of the active cone at 13,370 feet, where they were choked by sulphur fumes while a great column of steam rose thousands of feet into the sky. But the return journey took only one day, for they used the frozen slopes as slides, allowing their equipment to whisk down ahead of them.

Winter was a busy time for the scientists, and when spring came again, man-hauling parties sledged stores for the southern journey across the sea ice to Hut Point. Of the original ten ponies, two had died during the rough voyage in the *Nimrod*, and four from eating salt-impregnated gravel during the winter. Only four survived until the sledging season. The main depot-laying journey began on 22 September. The ponies did well on the Barrier, but the car proved of little use on the soft snow surfaces which were encountered some eight miles south of winter quarters. However, it hauled two sledges and six men as far as Inaccessible Island before it was abandoned. The man-hauling parties then established Depot A, 100 miles south of Hut Point.

Meanwhile a party of six under Professor David and including a young Australian, Douglas Mawson, set out for the South Magnetic Pole. This entailed climbing several glaciers to reach the high polar plateau, and as always in these early days, their rations were barely sufficient for the hard physical work they did. But on 18 January 1908 their compass needle pointed straight down into the Earth, and they knew they had reached their goal. The South Magnetic Pole, which moves its position over the centuries, was then found in latitude 72°25′S, longitude 155°25′E, at an altitude of 7260 feet.

The Southern Party consisted of Shackleton, Frank Wild, Lieutenant Adams, meteorologist, and Dr Marshall, surgeon and cartographer. They left Hut Point on 3 November, each of them leading a pony, and with a support party of

8. Shackleton's hut, Cape Royds

six men to haul loads for the first few days. They carried ninety days' supplies, and faced a return journey of 1704 statute miles. To reach the Pole their daily marches had to be three times as good as Scott's, and they relied on the ponies for meat, as well as to haul their sledges.

To begin with all went well. They passed through Depot A, and 100 miles south of it the first pony was shot, the meat being placed in Depot B. The Barrier surface was good and there was no wind. The sun was so hot that they pulled stripped to their shirts. To keep cool they chewed raw, frozen pony meat, but this did nothing to satisfy their terrible hunger pangs, for already they were half starved and dreaming about food. In the foothills of the mountains at the southern end of the Barrier, two more animals were killed and the meat depoted. Now they had to find a way through to the high plateau.

Leaving the last pony and the sledges in camp, the four men clambered across a stretch of ridges and crevasses, round an enormous chasm, and up a nearby peak some 3000 feet high. It was well worth the risks they had taken for they could now see for miles. All round them great mountains rose up, with sheer cliffs falling thousands of feet to a broad glacier which lay between them. This looked smooth and straight, and appeared to slope gently up to a great snow field on the plateau above. Here was the highway to the south. They named it the Beardmore Glacier, and hurried back for the sledges.

But in their weakening condition the ascent of the Beardmore was a terrible struggle. One day as they marched, Shackleton heard a sudden cry of 'Help!' and turning round he was horrified to see the pony sledge sticking up out of a crevasse. Wild was hanging on to it desperately, but the pony had disappeared. The sudden jerk of its fall had fortunately snapped the harness from the sledge. Otherwise Wild and the sledge would have followed it down into the abyss, and without the supplies lashed on this sledge the other three men would have died. As it was, the loss of this pony meat meant a serious reduction in their rations.

As the climb up the glacier continued, everyone in turn fell to the length of his harness into chasms 1000 feet deep. Each day wonderful new mountain peaks came into view, and had they not been so hungry they could better have appreciated the scenery. By Christmas Day they at last reached the top of the glacier and the edge of the plateau. They were 9500 feet above sea level, and the lack of oxygen caused them all to suffer blinding headaches and fits of giddiness. Their clothing was worn out, and their vitality so lowered by starvation that body temperatures fell four degrees below normal. Moisture from their breath, and running from their inflamed eyes, froze solid on to their faces and beards. No one thought of giving up, but by 2 January 1909 Shackleton was writing:

> God knows we are doing all we can . . . but we are not travelling fast enough to make our food spin out and get back to our depot in time . . . I must look at the matter sensibly and consider the lives of those who are with me.

On 9 January when Marshall made his observations they had reached latitude 88°23′S – only 97 miles from the Pole. For two days a blizzard had kept them tent-bound or they would have got even nearer. They could do no more. Here they planted the Union Jack given to them by Queen Alexandra, and turned back. Then began a 700 mile race with death to get home.

The descent of the Beardmore brought them to the limit of endurance. Fierce winds now howled behind them, and they hoisted a sail on the sledge. This sometimes rushed it down over ice falls and crevasses so fast that they could barely keep up, and the sledge became badly strained. Each depot was picked up only just in time as they arrived with empty food boxes.

By the time they had struggled back on to the Barrier, they were all suffering from dysentery – possibly through living on pony meat. At times they could not travel at all and were in great misery. Eating was a torment, for icy winds had blistered and burst their lips. But 15 February was the Boss's birthday and his companions had prepared a surprise; they gave him a cigarette made from the last shreds of their pipe tobacco, rolled in coarse paper.

Dr Marshall was now very ill, and by the end of the month he could not move. Leaving him in the tent with Adams and all the remaining food, Shackleton and Wild took one day's rations and a light sledge, and made a forced march back to Hut Point. Here they hoisted a flag which soon brought the *Nimrod* steaming round to their rescue. They had been out for 117 days.

They were welcomed aboard like men returned from the dead, for the captain had given them up for lost and was on the point of returning to New Zealand. Shackleton himself led the relief party which went out to fetch Marshall and Adams, and soon the expedition was safely embarked for home.

The *Nimrod* expedition discovered over 1000 miles of new land, and explored 200 miles of hitherto unknown coastline. The position of the South Magnetic Pole was fixed (*see map 4*), and Shackleton's Southern Party made a great advance towards the South Pole, traversing the largest valley glacier then known.

The Western Party under Brian Armytage explored 100 miles of the western mountains, where they found five new species of lichens, and 60 feet above sea level a raised beach full of recent shells. They brought back a large collection of photographs of the mountains and glaciers they had examined, and 250 lbs of rock specimens for analysis.

The scientific results were outstanding, and Shackleton returned to universal acclaim. Among the first to greet him was Captain Scott, who better than anyone could appreciate how much had been accomplished.

5
Scott's Last Expedition

When in 1910 it was announced that Captain Scott was to lead another Antarctic expedition, 8000 young men applied for a place. Dr 'Bill' Wilson, now his closest friend, was appointed Chief of the Scientific Staff, with young Apsley Cherry-Garrard as assistant zoologist. Three naval lieutenants included in the shore party were 'Teddy' Evans, the second-in-command, Victor Campbell and 'Birdie' Bowers. Captain 'Titus' Oates of the 6th Inniskilling Dragoons was in charge of the nineteen Manchurian ponies; Raymond Priestley was the geologist. Among the 12 ratings were three veterans of the *Discovery* expedition – Edgar Evans, William Lashly and Tom Crean.

On 15 June 1910 the expedition sailed for New Zealand in the *Terra Nova*. From there the voyage to McMurdo Sound was a terrible experience. A great storm did untold damage. As the ponies stood patiently on the heaving deck, 36-foot waves broke over them and three were lost. But they reached the Ross Sea in January 1911, and on a promontory later named Cape Evans they built their winter quarters (*see map 2*).

Scott had brought three motor sledges, but as they unloaded and drove the third one from the ship's side, the sea ice under it gave way and it was lost. This was the first of many blows to his plans for a polar journey.

As soon as men could be spared from building the hut, sledging operations began. While a geological party worked along the coastal mountains, the main effort was put into a depot-laying journey to support a party who would attempt to reach the Pole the following season. Twelve men, led by Scott himself, set out with 8 ponies and 26 dogs. The ponies pulled 900 lbs each and found it hard work when the sun made the surface sticky. Though they marched at 'night' to take advantage of colder temperatures, their feet often broke through the crust. The animals floundered up to their bellies in pockets of soft snow, but the party struggled on, and 30 miles from Hut Point they established Corner Camp. Here a blizzard forced them to lie up for three days. The dogs curled up snugly, allowing themselves to be drifted over, coming out only at meal times from warm, steaming holes. But the ponies suffered greatly; weakened by the cold, they were shaken and listless. Five days later Bluff Depot was established. Three of the animals could go no further, and had to be led back to base. The journey continued with five ponies and two dog teams, until 130 miles from Hut Point they put down One Ton Depot.

With only light loads, the return journey was easier. Much faster than the ponies, the dog teams ran ahead, covering as much as 17 miles a day. It was an exhilarating experience for the drivers until they found themselves among crevasses only 12 miles from Safety Camp. Suddenly all the middle dogs from Scott's team began disappearing through the ground. Two by two down they went, each pair howling and struggling in their harness as they fell. The leader, Osman, had crossed the crevasse safely. Now he stood on the far side, straining with all his might to take the weight of the dogs which had fallen through, while the sledge held them up from behind. The men ran the sledge across the gap, and Wilson hung on grimly to the anchored trace while the others began to haul the animals up and cut them out of their harness. Then Scott was lowered into the crevasse on a rope to rescue the last two dogs from a ledge 65 feet down. At this inopportune moment the loose dogs on the surface began a great fight with the second team tethered some distance away. Immediately there was uproar, and Scott found himself abandoned while his rope-tenders rushed off to sort out the mêlée. The next day they were back at Safety Camp.

While the depots were being laid, the *Terra Nova* had sailed along the Barrier, carrying the Eastern Party under Victor Campbell to King Edward VII Land. On arrival they found that a Norwegian expedition under Roald Amundsen was already established in the Bay of Whales. This was a bitter blow and Campbell returned to Cape Evans to inform his leader of the presence of his rival. He then decided to land his party as far north as possible in south Victoria Land, but ice conditions caused him to settle at Cape Adare.

When Scott returned to Safety Camp he found a letter from Campbell giving him this news. He wrote:

> Every incident of the day pales before the startling contents of the small bag which Atkinson gave me – a letter from Campbell setting out his doings and the finding of Amundsen established in the Bay of Whales. One thing only fixes itself definitely in my mind. The proper, as well as the wiser, course for us is to proceed exactly as though this had not happened. To go forward and do our best for the honour of our country, without fear or panic.
>
> There is no doubt that Amundsen's plan is a very serious menace to ours. He has a shorter distance to the Pole by 60 miles – I never thought he could have got so many dogs safely to the ice. His plan for running them seems excellent. But above and beyond all, he can start his journey early in the season, an impossible condition with ponies.

By February the season was drawing to a close. The sledging parties began returning to Hut Point, ready for the final journey across the sea ice to winter quarters at Cape Evans. Bowers, Cherry-Garrard and Crean, with four ponies each hauling a sledge, set off first. The sea ice was between 5 and 10 feet thick, and they camped for the night near the Barrier edge, well into the bay.

At 4.30 am Bowers awoke, and his diary tells a terrible story:

We were in the middle of a floating pack of broken-up ice . . . as far as the eye could see there was nothing solid; it was all broken up, and heaving up and down with the swell. Long black tongues of water were everywhere. The floe on which we were had split right under our picketing line, and cut poor 'Guts's' wall in half. 'Guts' himself had gone, and a dark streak of water alone showed the place where the ice had opened under him.

In great haste they packed up and harnessed the remaining ponies. Then they began jumping them from floe to floe, dragging the loaded sledges across the gaps.

Very little was said. Crean, like most blue jackets, behaved as if he had done this sort of thing often before. Cherry, the practical, after an hour or two dug out some chocolate and biscuit and distributed it . . . The ponies behaved as well as my companions and jumped the floes in great style . . .

Eventually they reached a point where a lead of water had opened between them and the Barrier edge. Here the sea was a boiling cauldron in which hundreds of killer whales swam about expectantly. It was impossible to get the ponies any further, and Crean was sent to fetch help.

Leaping from floe to floe as they churned their way out to sea, he worked his way to a point where the ice still ground against the Barrier. With the help of a ski stick he was seen to climb the Barrier face and disappear. Meanwhile Bowers and Cherry-Garrard spent a terrible day on the ice:

The Killers were too interested in us to be pleasant. They had a habit of bobbing up and down perpendicularly so as to see over the edge of a floe . . . The huge black and yellow heads, with sickening pig eyes only a few yards from us . . . As the day wore on skua gulls, looking upon us as certain carrion, settled down comfortably near us to await developments . . .

At 7 pm Crean at last reappeared at the Barrier edge with Scott and Oates. Letting down alpine ropes they dragged the two men off the floe and up to the top. Then the sledges were up ended on the floe, and used as ladders up the cliff; on this they could climb up and down from the Barrier. Soon they had hauled up all their gear, and only the ponies were left. At this moment the ice began to move again:

. . . like a black snake the lane of water stretched between the ponies and ourselves. It widened almost imperceptibly, 2 feet, 6 feet, 10 feet, 20 feet . . . Soon a lane 70 feet wide extended along the Barrier edge . . . Our three unfortunate beasts were some way out, sailing parallel to the Barrier . . . huddled together not the least disturbed, or doubting that we would bring them their breakfast nosebags as usual in the morning.

By morning all the ice had gone out to sea, but Bowers saw the floe, on which the ponies still stood, pushed up against the Barrier a mile away. The men rushed down to the ice once more in a desperate effort to lead them to safety. But they were only able to rescue one animal, the other two falling into the icy water between the floes.

Two other episodes must be mentioned briefly before the story of the polar journey. On 21 April the sun disappeared and just after mid-winter the strangest birds-nesting expedition of all time was organised. The large, dignified Emperor penguin is one of the most primitive birds known. In order that the chicks may have the whole summer in which to grow large enough to become self-sufficient, the parent birds are forced to incubate their eggs in the depths of the polar night. It was thought that a study of the embryo inside an unhatched egg might provide the missing link between birds and the reptiles from which they evolved. In order to obtain some eggs, on 27 June, Wilson, Bowers and Cherry-Garrard set out on an incredible winter journey.

The nearest known rookery was on sea ice inside a bay at Cape Crozier. This was guarded by great pressure ridges, crevasses and ice boulders which it would have been almost impossible to cross even in summer time. But hauling 253 lbs per man, they travelled over the sea ice and reached the Barrier in two days. Here temperatures fell to $-77°$F, moisture from their bodies froze their underwear and their anoraks solid, the rigid hoods preventing them from even turning their heads. It took many hours each day to make or break camp, and it became a nightly torture to force themselves painfully into iced-up sleeping bags.

The distance was some 60 miles. For two weeks they struggled across the coldest region, and then entered a windswept area where blizzard followed upon blizzard, until they reached the confused ice disturbances at the foothills of Cape Crozier. Here they climbed to 800 feet and chose what they thought would be a sheltered spot to pitch their camp. It took them two days to find enough stones to build the walls of a small hut in which they intended to make a blubber fire and live while they studied the habits of the penguins. A piece of canvas was lashed over the walls to form a roof, and their tent, full of gear, was pitched alongside the hut.

Their first attempt to clamber through the pressure ridges to the rookery failed, but the next day they managed to crawl through the ice disturbances down on to the sea ice. To obtain blubber for the stove they killed three penguins, and collecting six eggs they started back for their hut on the hillside.

That night a blizzard hit their camp. The heavy blocks of snow placed on the roof to hold down the canvas were carried away, and one tremendous gust of wind tore up the tent on which their lives depended. Inside the hut the men waited for their roof to vanish; after fourteen hours it did so, and snow began pouring in on them. With a gasp each man dived into his sleeping bag and remained there for the next forty-eight hours.

9. *Emperor penguin crêche, Cape Crozier*

When at last the wind fell they had their first piece of luck, for Bowers miraculously found the precious tent caught on a boulder nearby. But the journey back was even more dreadful. Sleeping bags which originally weighed 17 lbs each, had accumulated so much ice that they now weighed 40 lbs. On 2 August Scott wrote:

> The Crozier Party returned last night after enduring for five weeks the hardest conditions on record. They looked more weather-worn than anyone I have yet seen. Their faces were scarred and wrinkled, their eyes dull, their hands whitened and creased with constant exposure . . . Wilson is disappointed at seeing so little of the penguins, but to me, and to everyone who has remained here, the result of this effort is the appeal it makes to our imaginations as one of the most gallant stories of polar history . . .

An even worse ordeal befell the Northern Party. Towards the end of the second summer the *Terra Nova* landed Campbell, Priestley, Dr Levick and three seamen at Evans Cove, for what was intended to be a six-week geological excursion. But when the ship returned to pick them up again, a wide belt of pack ice blocked her way. All efforts to penetrate it failed, and by the end of February the party realised they were marooned. They had two worn tents, four weeks' skeleton rations, and summer clothing; and faced the prospect of five months of winter darkness before they would be able to sledge the 200 miles back to Cape Evans the following spring.

To survive, they dug a tunnel into a large snow drift and then excavated a cave 12 by 9 feet and 5 feet 6 inches high. They killed all the seals and penguins they could find, but it was a pitifully small supply, for it was late in the season and most had already left. All the pemmican and half the sledging rations were set aside for the journey back to base. A fireplace of stones was built in one corner of the cave, and they settled down to a winter of semi-darkness and slow starvation.

They ate blubber, cooked with blubber, and made blubber lamps out of Oxo tins and string. Their clothes and their sleeping bags became so soaked in blubber and blackened with soot that they stood up by themselves. Though they even ate the mustard plaster from the medical stores, for seven months they never had a full meal except on Midwinter Day. In turn they suffered from dysentery and ptomaine poisoning.

Every Saturday night they had a sing-song, and every Sunday they had 'church' and sang hymns from memory. A real red letter day was the occasion when they killed a seal and found 36 fish in its stomach: 'not too far digested to be still eatable'.

The following September six black ruffians emerged from their cave and loaded up the sledges. Two were very sick men, but they sledged for as long as they could keep on their feet; when they could do no more their companions put them on the sledge and hauled them back to Cape Evans. The journey took five weeks.

The Polar Journey

On 24 October 1911 the great journey to the Pole began. The motor party left first. Scott was eager that they should succeed for he hated the necessity to use animals, but one motor sledge broke down and was abandoned 14 miles from Hut Point, while the other was coaxed only as far as Corner Camp. From here the drivers man-hauled the loads. The ponies left next, and the dog teams last. Despite bad surfaces and high winds, by the middle of November the cavalcade had reached One Ton Depot.

Two weeks later a blizzard kept them tent-bound for five days. In fact this proved crucial to the whole journey; for while forced to lie up, they had to start eating the food intended for use beyond the Lower Glacier Depot, which they had not yet reached.

When the wind died down, the ponies were dug out and the cortege struggled on, not daring to stop for lunch for they knew the animals could never start again. For eleven hours they marched without a break, covering only 5 miles. But their last rest was near. Indeed, no one had expected the ponies to get as far as this.

At the Lower Glacier Depot the dog teams turned back, for it was thought that it would be impossible to get them over the crevasses and pressure ridges of the glacier. Three four-man parties went forward in harness, each hauling 800 lbs.

Almost at once the surfaces were terrible, and pulling was gruelling work. Sometimes after struggling for five hours they had advanced only half a mile.

> The sledges sank in over 12 inches . . . The tugs and heaves we enjoyed and the number of times we had to get out of our ski to upright the sledge were trifles compared with the strenuous exertion of every muscle and nerve to keep the wretched drag from stopping when once under way . . . We fairly played ourselves out, and finally had to give it up and relay.

Painfully they began the ascent of the Beardmore Glacier. By 19 December they were 1100 feet above sea level in wonderful mountain scenery. Two days later they built Upper Glacier Depot, after which the first supporting party turned back. Eight men continued the march: Scott, Wilson, Oates and Seaman Evans on the first sledge; Lieutenant Evans, Bowers, Lashly and Crean on the second.

To make up for the days lost through the last blizzard, they drove themselves to the limit. Rising at 5.45 am they were ready to leave camp at 7.15. They hauled for nine hours each day. Often it was clear and sunny, but the temperature never rose above zero. Once they reached the plateau a searing south wind always blew in their faces. On Christmas Day Lashly was forty-four, and there is a rueful entry in his diary:

> We have done 15 miles over a very changing surface. First of all it was very much

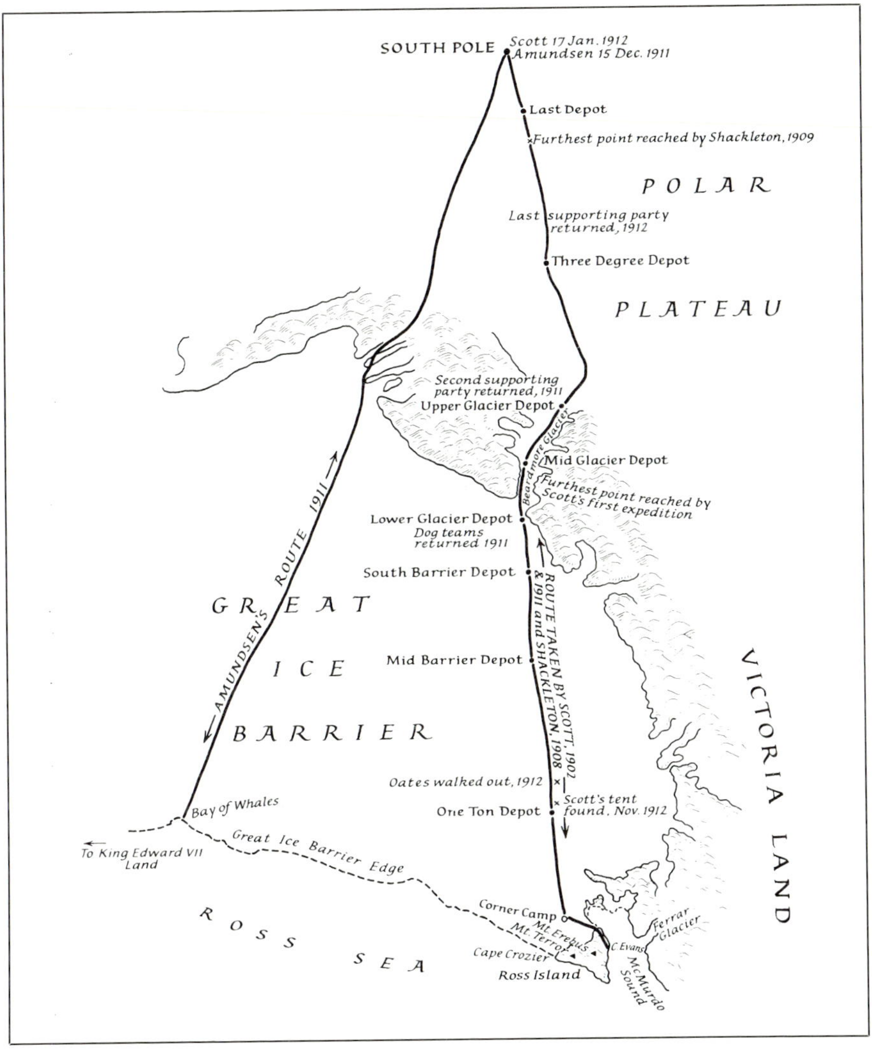

Map 2. Early routes to the Pole

crevassed and pretty rotten . . . I had the misfortune to drop clean through, but was stopped with a jerk when at the end of my harness. It was not of course a very nice sensation, especially on Christmas Day . . . Anyhow Mr Evans, Bowers and Crean hauled me out and Crean wished me many happy returns of the day, and of course I thanked him politely, and the others laughed.

Bowers takes up the story of the afternoon:

We had a great feed which I had kept hidden and out of the official weights . . . It consisted of a good fat hoosh with pony meat and ground biscuit; a chocolate hoosh made of water, cocoa, sugar, biscuit, raisins and thickened with a spoonful of arrow-root. Then came $2\frac{1}{2}$ square inches of plum-duff each, and a good mug of cocoa washed down the whole.

It was their last celebration. By the beginning of January all the men were seriously weakened, and the high altitude began to tell. Bowers wrote in his diary:

We are now over 10,000 feet above sea level. It makes it bad as we don't get enough heat in our food and the tea is not strong enough to run out of the pot. Everything gets cold so quickly, the water boils at about 196°F.

But Scott's great drive and nervous energy kept them all going until 4 January when the last supporting party turned back. They had reached latitude 87°32′S – it was 148 miles to the Pole.

When all had contributed so much to the venture, Scott found it heart-rending to decide who should turn back. He had planned to take four men to the Pole, and the rations were organised in four-man units. For some reason he changed his mind and Bowers now joined the polar party. Lieutenant Evans, Lashly and Crean saw them set off, and turned back for home, suffering a gruelling journey that nearly cost Evans his life.

The polar party marched forward in high spirits. The sun shone, and it was now virtually certain that they must reach their goal. Scott was confident that he had picked the right men for the final assault.

It is impossible to speak too highly of my companions . . . Wilson, tough as steel on the traces, never wavering from start to finish . . . Evans, a giant worker with a really remarkable headpiece . . . Little Bowers remains a marvel – he is thoroughly enjoying himself . . . Oates had his invaluable period with the ponies; now he is a foot slogger and goes hard the whole time. I would not like to be without him either.

The surfaces became very bad and the whole party began to feel the cold. They were faced with sastrugi (fluted ridges carved out of the snow surface by the strong winds) and pulling, always heavy work, became a torture. They were 27 miles from the Pole.

The next day they came upon the tracks of dog teams:

10. *Scott's Party at the Pole.* l. to r. *Wilson, Scott, Oates, Evans, Bowers*

This told us the whole story. The Norwegians have forestalled us and are first at the Pole. It is a terrible disappointment, and I am very sorry for my loyal companions . . .

It was, indeed, the bitterest blow. But they continued the march, and on 17 January 1912 they reached the South Pole. The Norwegians had left a small tent. Inside it was a message stating that they had arrived there on 15 December, five weeks earlier.

They built a cairn and put up the Union Jack. Then Bowers took photographs while Wilson sketched the scene. Scott wrote:

Great God this is an awful place, and terrible enough for us to have laboured to it without the reward of priority . . . Well, we have turned our back now on the goal of our ambition, and must face our 800 miles of solid dragging . . .

They turned back with relief. The wind was behind them so they fixed a mast and sail to the sledge and 'fairly slithered along before a fresh breeze'. But these happy conditions didn't last long. All the men were now very cold, and though each depot was picked up, they were very hungry.

But they were scientists to the end. As they came down through the mountains they could not bear to pass by the exposed rock face without stopping to collect some specimens:

> We all geologised till supper, and I was very late turning in, examining the moraine . . . magnificent Beacon Sandstone cliffs. Masses of limestone in the moraine, and dolerite crags in various places. Coal seams at all heights in the sandstone cliffs and lumps of weathered coal with fossil vegetable. Had a regular field day and got some splendid things in the short time.

Evans suffered continual frostbite, and had twice fallen into crevasses striking his head. Gradually he became dull and incapable, and when they left the Upper Glacier Depot he was detached from the sledge to march at his own pace. Near the bottom of the Beardmore he finally collapsed and died.

The four remaining men got safely back on to the Barrier, but now they were all weakening rapidly. Quite unexpectedly the temperature suddenly dropped to the minus thirties by day, the minus forties at night. By 6 March Titus Oates was unable to pull and realised that his condition was jeopardising the safety of his companions. He marched alongside the sledge for another four days, and then proposed that they should abandon him in his sleeping bag. This they all refused to do. That night he fell asleep hoping never to wake, but when morning came a slight blizzard was blowing and there was much drift. He said quietly, 'I'm just going outside for a minute' – and they never saw him again. In his distress Scott wrote:

> Should this be found I want these facts recorded . . . We can testify to his bravery. He has borne intense suffering for weeks without complaint, and to the very last was able and willing to discuss outside subjects. He did not – and would not – give up hope till the very end . . . We all hope to meet the end with a similar spirit, and assuredly the end is not far. My companions are unendingly cheerful . . . and though we constantly talk of fetching through, I don't think any one of us believes it in his heart.

They marched on doggedly. By 21 March they were within 11 miles of One Ton Depot – and safety. They had left just two days' food and barely one day's fuel. But it would be enough, they could just get through.

That night the cruellest of all their many misfortunes overtook them. A blizzard began to blow – *and it lasted nine days.*

Their companions at base were deeply shocked when the days wore on and they realised that the polar party must have perished. The following spring a search party set out along the route to find them. On 12 November 1912, just south of One Ton Depot, they saw a bamboo sticking up out of the snow, and underneath it they found the tent. All three men seemed to be sleeping peacefully.

Gently the relief party removed the bamboos, and the tent dropped down to cover them. Over it a great cairn was built and their friends put up a cross made from two skis. They brought back all the diaries, personal papers, and scientific records – and 30 lbs of geological specimens which had been carried to the very end.

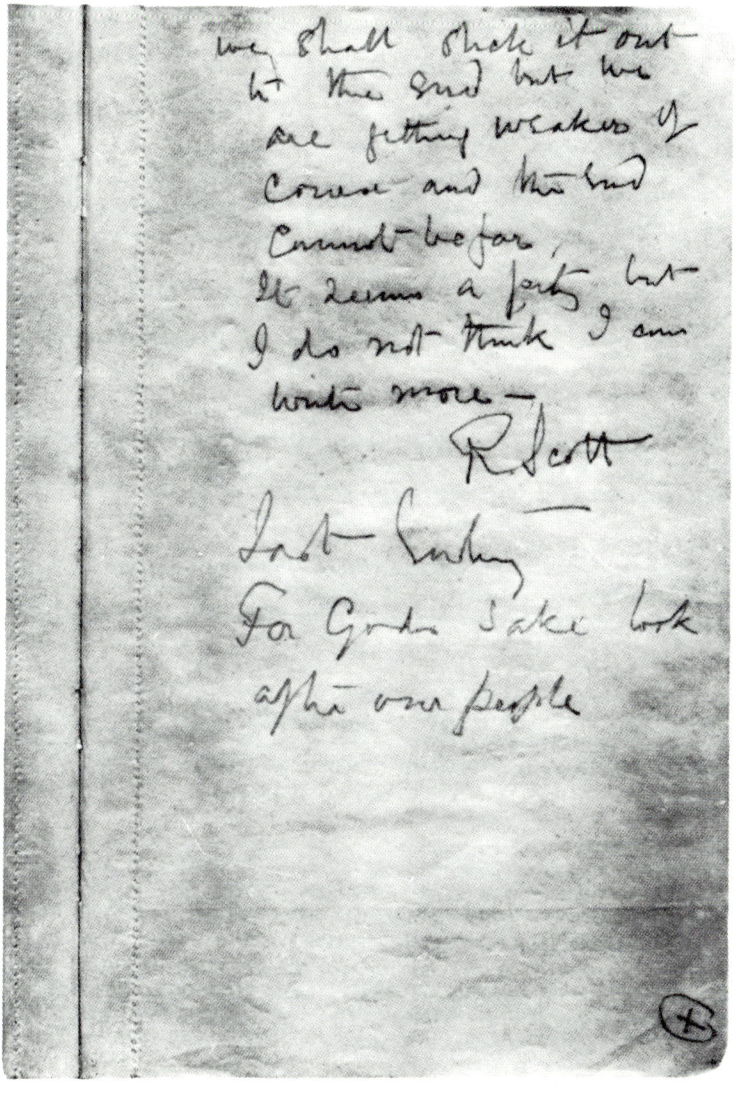
We shall stick it out
to the end but we
are getting weaker of
course and the end
cannot be far,
It seems a pity but
I do not think I can
write more –
R. Scott
Last Entry
For God's sake look
after our people

11. The last entry in Scott's journal

6

Roald Amundsen

Since his earliest years Roald Amundsen's consuming interest had been the Arctic. He was born into a Norwegian shipping family, and when both his parents died before he was twenty-two, he threw up his medical studies to go to sea. Eight years later he was in the Antarctic as First Mate of the *Belgica*.

Later he led an expedition to the North Magnetic Pole, and then discovered the long-sought North-West Passage, through the islands off the north coast of Canada into the Arctic Ocean. His most cherished dream was to be the first man to reach the North Pole. But while he was still raising the money and planning such an expedition, two Americans, Dr Frederick Cook and Robert Peary, each led parties to the Pole and claimed to have succeeded in reaching it.

Amundsen realised that a third expedition to the same place could only be an anti-climax. At the very last moment, and in complete secrecy, he switched his plans. Even the ship's company of the *Fram* at first thought they were sailing north; but when Amundsen reached Australia he sent a message to Scott, already on his way to McMurdo Sound, saying that he too was coming south.

The *Fram* arrived in the Bay of Whales in the summer of 1910. Till then no one had considered it a justifiable risk to build a base on the Great Ice Barrier itself, for fear that it would calve off and go out to sea. But Amundsen was an expert on ice. He had noticed that since the days of James Clark Ross, the Barrier ice in the Bay of Whales had never moved; he was sure that it must rest on land or shoals at this point, and he had the courage to establish his winter quarters, Framheim, on it. This put him 60 miles nearer the Pole than Scott's party at Cape Evans. He knew the British expedition intended to use the Beardmore Glacier to reach the polar plateau, and he gambled on finding an alternative route through the mountain ranges.

The Norwegians understood dogs far better than the British. They were the first to appreciate that when properly fed and managed, they are one of the most efficient means of travelling in Antarctic conditions. Amundsen brought with him 116 Greenland huskies. He was also the first Antarctic explorer to understand the importance of fresh meat to ward off scurvy. Before winter set in the Norwegians had stockpiled 60 tons of seal meat.

*

Amundsen's only objective was to reach the Pole – and if possible to get there first. Unhampered by the demands of any kind of scientific programme, his chosen companions were all expert skiers, dog-drivers and ice-craftsmen.

As soon as the ship was unloaded and the hut built, three long journeys were made to lay depots as far as latitude 82°S, and 3 tons of food were placed along the route. During the last of these journeys the weather was terrible and the surfaces very bad. Eight dogs were lost and the men were brought to the limit of endurance, but as Amundsen later wrote, 'This was the only dark memory of our stay in the south'.

In the southern spring of 1911 the polar journey began. Reading about the success of the dog teams, it is terrible to remember Scott's choice of ponies and the heart-breaking exertions of his man-hauling parties. In normally good conditions the Norwegians easily covered between 17 and 25 miles in a day. With light loads, and with their heads towards home, the dogs ran even faster. On one occasion the teams covered 62 miles in the day. The men never had to pull.

On 19 October Amundsen and four companions set out across the Barrier with four sledges and fifty-two dogs. For the first 100 miles surfaces were so good that the men rode on the sledges. When the great mountain ranges came into view the highest peaks rose to some 15,000 feet, but the Norwegians were thankful to see that they were seamed by a number of glaciers. They could hope that some would lead south.

They found, though, that there was no straight path up to the plateau. Many small glaciers filled the valleys, twisting and turning in every direction. As the teams climbed to the top of one, they found themselves descending many hundreds of feet into a valley beyond. This in turn brought them to the foot of another steep incline. Some of the ascents were so difficult that the sledges jerked forward a foot at a time; the dogs had to struggle hard to keep moving. Over and over again they strained into their harness, forcing the sledges forward yard by yard, while the drivers toiled with them, yelling encouragement. On one terrible morning of this kind of work they gained only 70 yards.

To add to their difficulties the crevasses became so numerous that they were finally forced to camp. Leaving the dogs tethered, the men went forward on skis trying to find a way out of the network of chasms. When they had found a route it required a tremendous effort to extricate themselves. Double teams of twenty-four dogs were harnessed to each sledge before the loads could be hauled. They were continually forced off course, and found themselves on a second plateau, with still more mountains ahead.

Here they rested their animals for four days, and a great many of the stores were depoted for the return journey. Twenty-four of the weakest dogs were killed to provide food for the remainder. The journey continued in the teeth of a blizzard, which perhaps only tough Scandinavians could have faced. At last they came to what they called the Devil's Glacier, because it was a fearsome place of jagged ice fields with crevasses everywhere. They could feel the vibration, and hear the thunder of avalanches crashing down from the peaks above. But it led them up on to the plateau.

Their troubles were virtually over. The dogs sped on in fine fettle, and of their last camp, only 15 miles short of their goal, Amundsen wrote, 'The atmosphere in the tent that night was like the eve of some great festival'. On 15 December 1911 they were the first men to reach the South Pole. They remained there for three days, resting the dogs, checking and re-checking their position. They were determined to make sure they had reached the one place on Earth from where every direction leads north.

While the main objects of Scott's expedition were scientific, the attainment of the Pole was a great personal ambition. Amundsen came south with only one idea, and took the prize. Yet ironically enough he wrote later,

> I cannot say . . . that the object of my life was attained . . . I had better be honest and admit straight out that I have never known any man to be placed in such a diametrically opposite position to the goal of his desires as I was at that moment. The regions around the *North* Pole . . . have attracted me from childhood, and here I stood at the *South* Pole. Can anything more topsy-turvy be imagined?

The return journey began, the dogs 'going like the wind', and after only 51 days on the land they were back on the Barrier ice. On 25 January 1912 their 11 surviving dogs brought them safely back to base.

The party were in high spirits as they went aboard the *Fram* the next day, only to find that no one in the ship liked to ask the question that was on all their minds. The five men who had conquered the Pole felt it might be considered boasting to mention it. So they all stood about nervously making conversation. At last someone cleared his throat and inquired casually, 'Well – been there?' Suddenly Amundsen and his companions were all roaring with laughter and gasping out their great news. Everyone started yelling with delight and thumping everyone else on the back. It was a wonderful welcome home.

On the same evening Scott was writing:

> Oates suffers from a very cold foot; Evans' fingers and nose are in a bad state, and tonight Wilson is suffering tortures from his eyes . . .

It was a story of high adventure and great courage. It was also a masterpiece of good organisation. Amundsen had a peculiar genius, based on sound knowledge of ice, which nerved him to take risks which could easily have spelt disaster. He achieved what was then thought impossible – he got dogs up the glaciers and across the high plateau.

In the course of their expeditions Scott took 23 scientists and technicians

12. *Amundsen's tent at the Pole, found by Scott five weeks later*

south, Shackleton took 22 and they brought back an enormous amount of data. Soundings taken from their ships produced charts, while the running surveys along the coast and the topographical surveys inland gave us the first outlines of a map. Physicists, geologists, meteorologists and biologists – all gleaned a rich harvest of knowledge.

The pity was that the plan for Amundsen's great journey had not included any scientific studies to advance our knowledge. Though the party got back well before the end of the season, with plenty of food remaining in the depots, it achieved nothing geographically or scientifically. Framheim was not a scientific station, and only limited meteorological records were kept. From the information brought back it was not even possible to draw an accurate map of the route which had been so courageously pioneered.

Nevertheless, it is interesting to note how each successive expedition got nearer to the Pole:

Date	*Name*	*Latitude South*	*Miles from Pole*
1774	*Cook*	71°10′	1130
1823	*Weddell*	74°15′	945
1842	*Ross*	78°09′	711
1902	*Scott*	82°17′	463
1909	*Shackleton*	88°23′	97
1911	*Amundsen*	90°00′	0
1912	*Scott*	90°00′	0

7
The Imperial Trans-Antarctic Expedition

There was one great polar challenge left – the first crossing of Antarctica, and Sir Ernest Shackleton was the man to accept it. His plan was for a support party from McMurdo Sound to lay depots southwards towards the Pole, while the main party under his personal command would cross the continent from a base on the Weddell Sea.

The Weddell Sea is a huge embayment, almost 1000 miles deep and 1000 miles across, bounded by land on three sides. Strong currents moving clockwise constantly churn the sea ice in a slow gyrating mill, and when winds force it against the land, tremendous pressure is built up. This buckles the floes, piling them one upon another, or causing them to rear up in great jagged masses, which can grow to towering heights as the ice jostles for room in the land-locked areas. In 1823 Weddell was fortunate to find open water, but later expeditions such as the Scottish National Antarctic Expedition led by Dr William Bruce in 1902, and the German expedition of 1911 under Dr Wilhelm Filchner, were frustrated by impenetrable fields of pack ice.

Shackleton himself, now 40 years old, sailed in the *Endurance* from South Georgia on 5 December 1914, with his old friend Frank Wild as second-in-command. Many tons of coal were stacked amidships and 69 huskies were tethered forward. A ton of whale meat hung in the rigging. It dripped blood constantly, keeping the dogs in a state of frenzy hoping that a morsel might fall their way. For two weeks the ship twisted and turned, carefully squeezing a way through the pack, and scraping past icebergs 150 feet high that towered well over her masts. Finally they were stopped by great ice cliffs which Shackleton named the Caird Coast, and turning due south they set course for Vahsel Bay.

Soon they were in a sea of mushy 'brash' ice which closed in round the ship ominously, and on 18 January 1915, only 60 miles from their goal, the wind packed ice tight round the *Endurance*, bringing her to a halt. As one of her crew wrote, she was 'frozen like an almond in the middle of a chocolate bar'. This chocolate bar was one million square miles of ice.

They fought for weeks to set her free. The ice round the ship was sawn up and great blocks of it were carried away to give her room to batter the floes ahead. But always more ice filled the gaps and it was the ship, not the floes, which got hurt. At the end of February they were forced to admit defeat

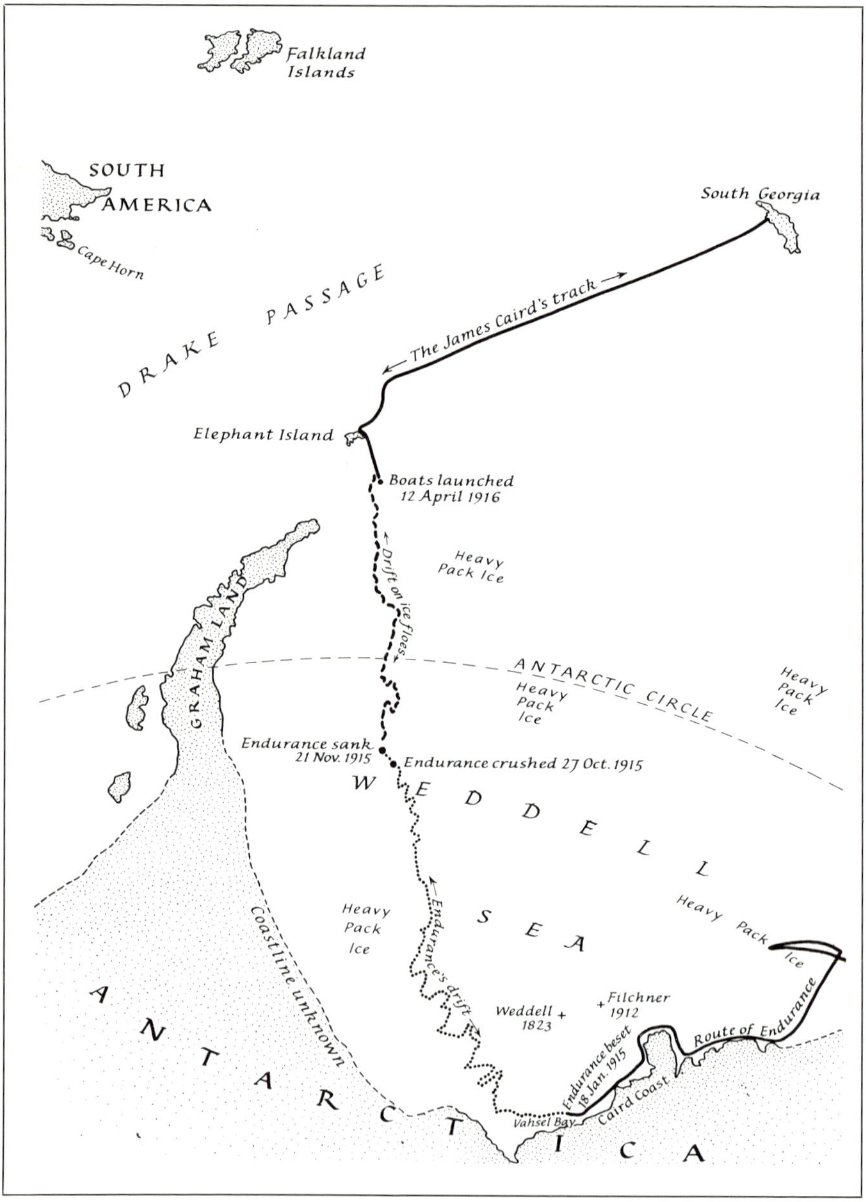

Map 3. Shackleton's track in the Weddell Sea

and abandon all hope of achieving their project. The boilers were let out and the *Endurance* became a winter scientific station.

Hunting parties went out to bring in all the seals they could find, and Frank Worsley, captain of the ship, watched uneasily as she drifted steadily into more congested ice. As long as the light lasted the men played hockey or football on the floes, but the sun left on 1 May and then their main recreation was to take the dog teams out on training runs. Crean began to train the pups in harness. He wrote:

> It was very amusing to see them with their rolling canter just managing to keep abreast by the sledge, and occasionally cocking an eye with an appealing look in the hope of being taken aboard for a ride.

On 15 July the wind suddenly began screaming through the rigging at gale force. Falling snow was blown into every cranny. On the windward side of the ship snowdrifts 14 feet high built up, weighing some 100 tons. The strain was beginning. The floes creaked and groaned as they ground against each other. As pressure built up, large chunks of ice were up-ended and thrown against the ship's side. But she rose up on top of the disturbance, and hung at an angle which varied as the ice hummocks supporting her changed their position.

Anxiety continued throughout the winter. In the last days of September the roar of the pressure grew louder. It was clear that stupendous forces were at work. Several times the ship was badly nipped. By 25 October Shackleton was writing:

> Heavy pressure ridges were forming in all directions . . . Huge blocks of ice, weighing many tons, were lifted into the air and tossed aside as other masses rose beneath them. We were helpless intruders in a strange world . . .

The end was inevitable. Two days later the *Endurance* was racked and twisted by the strain, leaking badly. The decks buckled, and sounds like pistol shots told them when the beams broke. Shackleton gave orders to abandon ship.

Two lifeboats and essential stores had already been placed on the ice some distance away, and here they pitched their first camp. The *Endurance* had drifted for 281 days. Now preparations were made to march to the edge of the pack, and their two boats, named *James Caird* and *Dudley Docker* after two of the expedition's benefactors, were mounted on specially built sledges. Each boat on its sledge weighed over a ton.

Each man was allowed to keep only 2 lbs of personal gear, and the Boss himself made the first gesture by emptying his pockets and tossing away his gold cigarette case and some sovereigns. But Leonard Hussey, the meteorologist, was ordered to take his banjo (though it weighed 12 lbs), for Shackleton well knew the value of a sing-song in the dark days to be faced.

13. Endurance *crushed in the Weddell Sea*

When they left her next morning the *Endurance* lay on her side, her masts broken and great fingers of ice sticking through her bulkheads. Four men went ahead carrying shovels and pickaxes to find a route along which the heavy boats could be hauled. Every few hundred yards, ridges had to be chopped away until they had carved a passage wide enough for the sledges. If a ridge was too high for this, they built an ice-ramp up one side and down the other. The dog teams followed, and lastly the boats, each hauled in turn by fifteen men.

It was killing work. On the first day they covered only $1\frac{1}{2}$ miles. The following morning Shackleton and Wild went forward to prospect the route, but all they could see ahead was a vast area of pressure ridges over which it would be impossible to move the laden sledges. Shackleton decided that they must remain on the floe they had reached until the drift carried them nearer to land. So they built Ocean Camp. Wild returned to the ship with the dog teams and brought up a third boat, the *Stancombe Wills*.

The party lived at Ocean Camp for two months, killing the rare seals as they appeared, but getting steadily more hungry:

14. *'They built Patience Camp on the largest floe . . .'*

All is eaten that comes to each tent, and everything is most carefully and accurately divided into as many equal portions as there are men in the tent. One member then closes his eyes or turns his head away and calls out the names at random, as the cook for the day points to each portion, saying at the same time 'Whose?'

On 6 November a blizzard struck from the south. Though it kept them in overcrowded tents and increased their miseries, it was welcomed for it increased their rate of drift. It was now high summer, and as the temperature rose a surface thaw set in. Their boots, clothes and sleeping bags were all soaked and sodden. They lived in a permanent state of squelchiness.

Two weeks later the *Endurance* disappeared:

. . . as we lay in our tents we heard the Boss call out 'She's going boys!' We were out in a second and up on the look-out station . . . and sure enough, there was our poor ship a mile and a half away struggling in her death agony. She went down bows first, her stern raised in the air. She gave one quick dive and the ice closed over her for ever . . .

Towards the end of December the ice around them began to rot. Shackleton decided that they must march on the 23rd, and since they would not be able to carry all the food with them, they celebrated Christmas Day on the 22nd, every man eating as much as he could. This 'gorgie' was the last full meal they had for eight months.

The expedition marched at night when the lower temperatures hardened the surface, and each day, while the men slept, Shackleton and Wild went forward on skis marking out the best route. One of the men described their conditions:

> It's a hard, rough, jolly life, this marching and camping; no washing of self or dishes, no undressing, no changing of clothes. We have our food anyhow, and always impregnated with blubber smoke; sleeping almost on the bare snow and working as hard as the human physique is capable of doing on the minimum of food.

But this second effort to march north only lasted seven days, during which they had advanced seven and a half miles. Once more they were hemmed in and forced to a halt by impassable pressure ridges. They built Patience Camp on the largest floe they could find, and they lived on it for the next three and a half months. By the end of January 1916 even seal meat was very scarce and five dog teams had to be shot.

> We only get one hot beverage a day . . . For the rest we have iced water. Sometimes we are short even of this, so we take a few chips of ice in a tobacco tin to bed with us. In the morning there is about a spoonful of water in the tin, and one has to lie very still all night so as not to spill it.

On 20 March they experienced the worst blizzard they had known. Thick powdery snow buried the camp, and the weakened men in torn greasy clothes were bitterly cold. But when the weather cleared and Worsley could take a sun sight, they had drifted 73 miles and were north of the Antarctic Circle.

At the end of the month the temperature rose to 33°F and rain fell. That night the watchman noticed a 'very distinct swell' gently lifting their floe. At 5.20 am it split. Everyone rushed from tents to see the crack slowly widening. Their precious meat pile was on the far side, and several men jumped the gap to throw it back over the open water. After that half the men watched the ice continuously, and those off duty slept fully dressed, ready for instant departure.

Within a few days a heavy swell was rolling through the pack, while everywhere cracks appeared in the floes. Patience Camp had become a triangular raft of ice, measuring roughly 90 by 100 by 120 yards across. It was impossible to stay there any longer. On 12 April the boats were eased into the water and loaded; the crews scrambled aboard and began to row with all their strength.

The next six days and nights were a nightmare during which Shackleton never once slept. Throughout the first day they rowed gingerly through the jostling ice floes and by evening had covered seven miles. Then they hauled the boats out on to a flat floe 200 yards across, and camped for the night. Towards midnight Shackleton, ever alert, felt uneasy. He dressed and went outside. As he stood in the darkness peering at the ice, the floe split right under the tent in which eight men were asleep. The tent collapsed and only seven men scrambled from under it. Shackleton dashed forward and dropped to his knees. In the crack of open water he could faintly make out a sleeping bag, from which he heard gasping noises. Reaching down he gave one tremendous heave and pulled the bag out on to the ice. Seconds later the two halves of the floe crashed together again. Further sleep was out of the question. The stove was lit for a hot drink of weak powdered milk. To prevent the half-drowned man from freezing to death in his sodden clothes, for the rest of the night men took turns walking up and down with him. His clothes crackled as they forced him to keep moving, and they could hear the tinkle of the ice crystals that fell from him.

On the second day they rowed through the leads of open water until they found themselves in a choppy sea. Sails were hoisted, but as soon as the boats left the comparative protection of the pack, they were struck by the full force of a high wind and breaking seas. They were forced to turn about and return to the ice.

That evening they found a 'floe-berg': a thick mass of old blue pressure ice about 35 yards square, which rose in places 15 feet above the water. It had been eroded by the sea around the waterline, and an overhang of rotten ice rose up 5 feet out of the water. Superhuman efforts were needed to haul the boats up on to this precarious platform. After a supper of dog pemmican, powdered milk and two lumps of sugar, the men crawled into sodden sleeping bags, praying that the berg would last the night.

The wind rose to gale force, blowing quantities of pack ice all round them. Great rollers 30 feet high swept through the pack, lifting their frail camp to the crest of each succeeding wave, then dropping it into the valleys between. By dawn on the third day it was clear that their floe-berg would up-end at any moment and cast them into the cauldron of fragmented ice. Yet it was impossible to launch the boats.

With only three hours of daylight left, suddenly a pool of water began forming just beside the camp. The men literally pitched the boats off the floe, stores were thrown aboard and the crews dropped down after them. Once more they were rowing with all their might. The wind had abated, and soon they were able to hoist sail. In the last glimmer of light they secured the boats alongside another floe, but never again would they camp on rotting ice.

Only the cook and his mate (now so black with blubber smoke that they were known as 'Potash and Pearlmutter') landed with the blubber stove to prepare supper. When they had eaten, the boats were roped together to prevent them becoming separated, and they rowed through the night. Each man was given a turn at the oars as often as possible, for it was the best way to keep warm. The others huddled together, clasped in each other's arms, trying to generate a little heat despite their frozen clothing. In the morning they set sail again in open water, but by nightfall on the fourth day they could not even find a floe large enough to allow the cook to land. Cold sledging ration was issued, and there were no hot drinks. The men shivered uncontrollably, their eyes bloodshot from lack of sleep, their beards encrusted in ice.

By noon on the fifth day they reached the true edge of the pack and found themselves spewed into the open sea. The swell, which up till now had been damped by ice, produced huge rollers which met them head on. The small boats climbed to the crest of each one and then began the steep descent; the men clung to the sides, desperately baling out the water which threatened to sink them. It had happened so suddenly that there had been no time to take ice into the boats for drinking water. They became tortured by thirst.

When darkness fell, Shackleton knew that on no account must the boats become separated. He dared not sail through the night for fear that they might miss the only land ahead of them. In such an event they could be carried straight out into the south Atlantic, where they would never be able to beat back against the prevailing currents. The *Dudley Docker* rigged an improvised sea anchor, and roped together they hove-to in line astern. When the sun rose on the sixth morning they could see Elephant Island dead ahead. Worsley, the navigator, had done a wonderful job.

All day they sailed or rowed through clear seas. The sun beat down from a cloudless sky which increased their thirst. Their mouths were too sore to eat. The next day they stumbled ashore on Elephant Island. It was only a small, bleak beach lying at the foot of high rocky cliffs and exposed to the fury of the ocean. But it didn't move under them. Seals lay basking a little distance away, and very soon the cook was frying an endless supply of steaks. A long intermittent meal went on as they pitched their tents, until every man had eaten all he could hold. Then they lay down and slept the sleep of utter exhaustion.

It was almost the end of April, the beginning of a second winter. No one would ever dream of looking for them on the shores of Elephant Island. If they were to be saved, Shackleton knew that he must go for help. The nearest land was the Falkland Islands or Cape Horn. But the prevailing winds blew towards South Georgia, more than 800 miles across the stormiest seas in the world.

Putting Frank Wild in charge of the main party, he picked Worsley as navigator and four of the strongest seamen to make the most remarkable boat voyage in history. The *James Caird* was stocked with six weeks' provisions and two barrels of fresh water, and after a few days' rest the six men set out.

15. *'The men piled into this dim cavern . . . like sardines in a tin'*

On their success depended the lives of the twenty-two left behind. They gave them three cheers as the boat disappeared, then turned to face the bleakness of waiting and the winter night.

Three of the party left behind were very sick men, none were fit for hard physical effort. But they had to have shelter. Under Wild's cheerful determination they slowly gathered sufficient large, flat stones from the other end of the beach to build two end walls 4 feet high. The *Dudley Docker* and the *Stancombe Wills* were turned upside down and laid lengthwise on them, and tent canvas was stretched right over the boats, to hang down and form the long side walls of a tiny hut. The blubber stove was placed in the centre, with its chimney rising up between the boats. The men piled into this dim cavern, their sleeping bags closely packed like sardines in a tin.

Many of them suffered from salt water boils and similar infections, and the two doctors had a steady flow of patients. The youngest seaman had had his feet so severely frostbitten during the boat journey that gangrene set in. Using their last 6 oz of chloroform the toes of his left foot had to be amputated. The mental state of the men caused Wild some anxiety as the weeks turned into months, and still the Boss did not come back. He had a hard time sustaining the spirits of some of them, particularly after the last pipeful of tobacco was finished.

As the seals and penguins left for warmer climes, food became very short. But Hussey still had his banjo, and Midwinter Day was celebrated in style with toasts drunk in 'Gut Rot 1916', a fearful mixture of water, sugar, ginger and methylated spirit from the Primus. Every morning someone climbed a nearby hill to look for the ship which would bring the Boss.

When August came and still no ship appeared even the stoutest optimists lost heart. Wild gave orders that every scrap of cord or wool and all sails were to be carefully preserved against the prospect of another boat journey. The men's diaries reflected their hardships and the fears they dared not voice:

> We are pretty short of both fuel and meat . . . Sir Ernest's non-return is now openly discussed . . .
>
> We have been eating seaweed lately, boiled. The taste is peculiar.
>
> . . . eagerly on the lookout for the relief ship . . . Some of the party have quite given up all hope of her coming . . .

The *James Caird* had sailed on 24 April, a tiny cockleshell in which six weakened and weary men dared to challenge a ruthless ocean. If Worsley's navigation was wrong and they missed South Georgia, the next stop was South Africa, 3000 miles farther on. For sixteen days and nights they faced tempestuous seas and fought a succession of gales. Cascades of foaming water rolled into the boat in icy streams until everything was wet through. As the temperature fell, the water turned to ice and the boat wallowed dangerously. The crew crawled round the slippery surface on all fours, chipping it away until she regained buoyancy – and there was not an oilskin between them.

On the rare occasions when they saw the sun, Worsley rushed for his sextant. In the bobbing boat he knelt on the helmsman's seat, two men holding him round the waist while he took his sights. Halfway through this dreadful ordeal the reindeer sleeping-bags began to rot. They had lost all their hairs long ago, now they became 'a hopeless, sloppy, slimy mess, smelling badly'. Their second barrel of water sprang a leak and became contaminated with salt. From then on thirst became a torment.

On the sixteenth weary day, when they had been 'pounded, bruised and drenched almost to the point of insensibility', they saw land dead ahead. Soon they could hear the rumbling of breakers as giant waves crashed on to the reefs. Great spumes of water shot upwards, and in despair they realised that it would be suicidal to land a boat. A last dreadful night had to be endured as they fought the suction of the ebbing tide in the teeth of a gale. But the next morning they found a narrow gap in the reef and ran the *James Caird* through it. She rose on a swell, her keel ground against the rocks, and Shackleton jumped ashore to secure the line. A stream of fresh water ran down from a nearby glacier.

But they had landed on the uninhabited side of South Georgia. Twenty-nine miles of high and steep mountains that had never been crossed lay between them and the whaling station at Stromness, and two of the party were too weak to face further hardships. Shackleton announced that one man would be left in charge of the invalids, while he, with Worsley and Crean, would go over the mountains for help.

After two days they had regained their strength sufficiently to sail to King Haakon Bay. Here hundreds of elephant seals lay basking on a gently sloping beach, and with a food supply assured, the *James Caird* was hauled up and turned over. When they had shored her up with a foundation of stones she made a fine shelter. They called their new home Peggotty Camp.

At 3 am on 19 May, Shackleton and his two companions set out in brilliant moonshine. They had no tent and even the sleeping-bags were left behind to save weight on this forced march. Each man carried three days' sledging ration. In addition they had one filled Primus, a small cooking pot and a few matches, two compasses, 50 feet of rope knotted together, and an adze which could be used as an ice axe. To strengthen their worn-out footwear the carpenter took out four dozen screws from the boat and drove eight into each boot.

The chart they carried showed only the coastline; the interior was a total blank. As dawn broke a thick fog rolled in, but soon a range of hills lay dead ahead, with four main peaks standing in line like sentinels. Twice they struggled by different routes up the ridges, only to find that the descent into the valley below was impossible. The third time, they reached the summit as light was fading and began a dangerously steep descent, bitterly chilled. After half an hour of carefully cutting steps in the ice, Shackleton realised that their rate of progress was futile. Unless they could get down quickly they would perish. He proposed that they should slide.

The Boss was known for his caution; Worsley and Crean were stunned. What if they hit a rock, or slid to the edge of another precipice? But there wasn't much choice. Untying the rope which joined them, each man sat down and coiled his share of it to form a mat. Shackleton led, with Worsley clinging to his waist and Crean latched on behind. They shot forward, increasing speed rapidly, with the wind shrieking round them. Within minutes the slope levelled off and suddenly they came to a halt in a snow bank. They had done it! As they prepared a meal in the valley, the ridge they had just left 2000 feet above disappeared in thick fog.

Throughout the night they picked a cautious route through a belt of crevasses by the light of a full moon. By 5 am they could hardly move their legs and were forced to rest behind a rock. Huddling together for warmth Worsley and Crean immediately fell asleep. The Boss had promised them half an hour, but in that time they could all freeze into gentle oblivion. After five minutes he jerked them awake, assured them that half an hour had passed and it was time to move. As the sun rose over the mountains, they could see a clear path through a valley, beyond which lay the hills to the west of Stromness. At 6.30 am in the clear air they heard faintly the factory whistles which wakened the men at the whaling station. All the morning they marched, and by 1.30 pm they stood at last on a ridge looking down on Stromness 2500 feet below. The final descent ended in a ravine where they found themselves wading knee-deep through a small stream which narrowed to a waterfall. There was no way round – they had to drop down through it. Making one end of the rope fast to a boulder, Crean was lowered, gasping and spluttering through the icy water. The others followed, and dripping wet they set off on the last mile to the station.

Seldom can three such filthy, unkempt castaways have returned to civilization. In South Georgia the crew of the *Endurance* had been given up for lost. Two small boys who were the first to see them fled in terror. Their hair was down to their shoulders, their eyes deeply sunk and reddened with salt, their beards stiff with blubber oil, their clothes in rags. They smelt terrible.

The whaling foreman watched their slow approach hardly able to believe his eyes, for *they came from the wrong direction.* Workmen stopped to stare as the first ragamuffin asked politely in English to be taken to the factory manager. His house was a hundred yards away, and when he answered the knock on his door he stared in shocked amazement.

'Who are you?' he enquired at last.

'My name is Shackleton', replied the voice from the dead.

The whalers were wonderful. Some of the Norwegian skippers had sailed the Antarctic seas for thirty years, and of all people they could appreciate the extraordinary skill and courage of the six men who had brought a 22-foot open boat across the Drake Passage to safety. Nothing was too much trouble for them. That evening the catcher *Samson* took Worsley round the island to Peggotty Camp. The three men, waiting there for relief, were at first hurt that none of their companions had bothered to come back for them. Until he actually spoke they had not recognised Worsley clean shaven, with short hair and fresh clothes.

Meanwhile Shackleton was already arranging for the rescue of the party on Elephant Island. Four successive relief expeditions were organised, but each time great storms and belts of pack ice prevented the ships from reaching the island. Finally the *Yelcho*, lent to Shackleton by the Chilean Government, succeeded, four months and six days after the party had been left.

It was lunch time, and the marooned men now had only two days' food left. As they were sitting down to a hoosh of boiled seal's backbone, limpets and seaweed, one of them who had been up to the look-out post came tearing into the hut gasping 'Ship O!'

16. *'Again and again we cheered . . .'*

Before there was time for a reply there was a rush of members tumbling over one another, all mixed up with mugs of seal hoosh, making a simultaneous dive for the door hole which was immediately torn to shreds . . . members who could not pass through it on account of the crush, made their exit through the 'wall' or what remained of it.

As the *Yelcho* dropped anchor,

Again and again we cheered, though our feeble cries could certainly not have carried so far . . . a boat was lowered, and we could recognise Sir Ernest's figure as he climbed down the ladder . . . We intend to keep August 30th as a festival for the rest of our lives.

Despite its epic quality this expedition was a disaster. Yet it produced scientific results of considerable value. The discovery of 300 miles of new land, and the continuous soundings from the ship throughout her 1000 mile drift, contributed much to the charting of the Weddell Sea and its coastline. The drift of the *Endurance* also added considerably to our knowledge of oceanography, meteorology and the glaciology of the pack ice. Much was learnt about the salinity of the sea, while the regular dredgings brought up a wealth of material of interest to biologists. But perhaps Shackleton's greatest achievement was that he brought his party back to safety without the loss of a single human life. So ended the heroic era.

8

Australasian Activities

Since the early days of the heroic age, Australian explorers had been taking part in all the major British expeditions. The first Australian to go south, in 1898, was Louis Bernacchi, a physicist and a member of C. E. Borchgrevink's *Southern Cross* expedition. The party established a base at Robertson Bay beside Cape Adare (*see map 4*), at the same time that de Gerlache was beset in the *Belgica*, and was the first expedition ever to winter on the continent. Later, Bernacchi also took part in Scott's *Discovery* expedition.

Douglas Mawson, one of the greatest of Australian explorers, was a member of Shackleton's expedition which established the position of the South Magnetic Pole. After his return to Australia, Mawson set about organising the largest and best equipped scientific team that had yet been promoted. Their aim was to explore the little known sector of the Antarctic continent immediately to the south of Australia. Some seventy years before, an American expedition under Wilkes and a French expedition under Dumont d'Urville had sailed in these waters. d'Urville had sighted land at a point almost due south of Tasmania, which he had named Adélie Land in honour of his wife. In 1902 a German expedition landed a party some 1500 miles further west. But apart from these excursions, the whole coastline as far east as Cape Adare, where Scott's parties worked, was entirely unknown.

The Australasian Antarctic Expedition of 1911 sailed from Hobart in the *Aurora*, and established its main base at Cape Denison. This was a bleak area, where the unbroken ice sheet rose sharply to 3000 feet, and blizzards poured down continually from the high plateau. The hut, anchored to the ice and strongly lashed down, shook like a leaf; inside, the roar of the wind often made normal conversation impossible. Outside, men leaning into the gale bent almost double as they struggled across to the meteorological screen to read the instruments. If the blast stopped suddenly for a few seconds, they fell flat on their faces.

This was the first expedition ever to be equipped with radio, and a relay station was established on Macquarie Island, whence messages could be transmitted to Melbourne. But there was no portable equipment to maintain touch with field parties.

Among their exploratory journeys was an unforgettable one led by Mawson himself, with Lieutenant B. E. S. Ninnis and Dr Xavier Mertz. On 10 November

1912, they set out with two dog teams and nine weeks' food, to examine the coastline eastwards to Cape Adare.

In a month they had covered 300 miles. Travelling over a good surface which gave no indication of danger, Ninnis and his team suddenly disappeared into a crevasse and were never seen or heard again. His horrified companions tied together all their available rope, but its total length was insufficient to reach the bottom of the chasm. For hours they shouted into the abyss, but no sound came back. With Ninnis had gone the strongest dog team, most of the provisions, their tent, and all the dog food. They were left with six dogs and food for one and a half weeks.

Deeply shocked, Mawson and Mertz started the race back on starvation rations; eating their dogs as each in turn died, the remainder being fed on a few rawhide straps. The animals became but bags of bones with virtually no nourishment value. Their meat was so stringy that even after hours of boiling it was still unchewable, and the men found it revolting. The only small bonus was the dogs' livers; these did not shrink with starvation and normally weighed about 2 lbs each. This they regarded as their life-line.

Mertz fitted a spare tent cover over a make-shift frame consisting of his own skis and two lengths of sledge runner lashed together at the apex. Inside there was just room for two sleeping bags but neither man could rise above a sitting position.

Gradually sledging without food in the bitter cold took its toll and their bodies began to rot. They became dizzy and stumbled about suffering from nausea. Their hair fell out, their skin split and peeled off in strips, leaving raw patches which were rubbed sore.

Halfway home Mertz began to suffer violent stomach pains and could hardly travel at all; some days they only covered two miles. Mawson decided on two days' rest in the tiny 'tent' hoping he might recover – knowing that this would prejudice his own chances of survival. But Mertz got worse, having to be helped in and out of his bag, and suffering from dysentry. On the third day Mawson forced him up and managed to haul him onto the sledge, but after only two and a half miles the sick man was so chilled that they had to camp again. Several times that day he fell into what looked like fits and was unaware of his surroundings.

By 7 January 1913 Mertz was shouting in delirium, his arms thrashing wildly around the confined space. Mawson was forced to sit on his chest as he struggled to quieten his dementia. By midnight he lay in a coma. Mawson, physically and emotionally drained, crawled into his own wet bag and tried to sleep. At 2 am he awoke – there was no sound from his companion and he reached out to touch him. Xavier Mertz had mercifully died.

Very little was known about vitamins in those days. It was another eight years before a substance in which dogs' livers are particularly rich was isolated as vitamin A. Yet another twenty years was to pass before it was recognised that excessive quantities of vitamin A could cause biological havoc in man. With six dogs to live on, these two men had consumed sixty toxic doses of this, which in fact was the cause of Mertz's terrible death. It was not the result of a breakdown in his courageous personality but the result of what is now clinically described as Hypervitaminosis A.

A few hundred miles away, during the previous season, Scott and his party had also been struggling home with a sick comrade who likewise died. They, too, had not realised the importance of vitamins in their diet, and malnutrition had started as soon as they began their journey to the Pole.

Mawson then faced the last 100 miles back to base alone. Sawing the sledge in half with a pocket knife, he discarded the rear section, erected a crude mast and hoisted a sail made from an old waterproof clothes-bag and a Burberry. He never expected to win through, but he was determined to reach the farthest possible point before he gave up. Once he fell the length of his harness into a hidden crevasse, but the sledge jammed on the surface and held him. As he climbed painfully up the wall of the chasm, a cornice gave way and he dropped down again. By a supreme effort he clambered out a second time, lay exhausted on the surface and fainted. An hour later, numb with cold, he regained consciousness and managed to erect his tent.

Now very sick and emaciated, but helped by the sail on the sledge, he struggled a little further each day, until at last his luck turned: he saw a food bag which had been left on a cairn by the rescue party which was out looking for him. Only five and a half miles from base, the wind started to blow at hurricane force, filling the air with drift. He was tent-bound for a week, during which the *Aurora* arrived to evacuate the expedition. On 8 February, he finally staggered into the hut, to find that the ship had sailed that very morning and was a speck on the horizon. But five of his men had remained behind to spend a second winter with him. It was two months before they nursed him back to strength. During the two years this expedition spent in the field, 1840 miles of new land or ice shelf was seen and charted.

After the end of the First World War interest in Antarctica revived, and a number of countries organised expeditions. Sir Douglas Mawson, and many scientific societies in Australia, constantly pressed the government to play its part in the new era of exploration, but it was not until 1929 that Mawson was able to consolidate the scientific work of his earlier expedition. In that year, under his leadership the British-Australian-New Zealand Antarctic Expedition (BANZARE) spent the summer working along the coast of Australian Antarctic Territory, and the region was claimed for the Crown. For this venture Scott's ship *Discovery* was modified to carry a seaplane which was used successfully for ice reconnaissance. Princess Elizabeth Land was seen from

17. Mawson Station, the first ANARE *base, built in 1954*

the air, while parties were landed at a number of points where annexation ceremonies were carried out.

Due largely to profitable whaling activities, in which the Norwegians played a major part, political rivalry was developing and territorial claims were put forward, sometimes on the flimsiest of pretexts. Australia had no wish to see control of the sector nearest her shores pass into the hands of another power, and realised that formal claims had to be backed up by occupation. In 1947, again under pressure from Mawson, a plan was finally approved to establish permanent stations in the Australian quadrant. So the Australian National Antarctic Research Expedition (ANARE) was born.

During the first phase, HMAS *Labuan* was used to establish bases on Heard Island and Macquarie Island. There were constant snow squalls, and gales blew at 120 mph, but despite the difficulties, four huts were erected and fourteen men were left to man the stations.

18. Scott Base, McMurdo Sound

At Macquarie Island, sheep and goats were landed and provided a useful supplement to the men's diet. Later a cow was added to the farmyard. She calved successfully and produced 820 gallons of milk, which made it possible to produce butter for the first time in the Antarctic. The only problem was that in snowy weather she became iced up and had to be 'defrosted'.

In 1954, the Danish ice-strengthened ship *Kista Dan* was chartered to relieve the island stations and to establish the first permanent base on the continent itself. She had great difficulty in forcing a passage through heavy pack ice and was twice beset for days at a time. The site chosen for the new station, Mawson, was a rocky area on the westerly coast of Australian Antarctic Territory. The *Kista Dan* carried two small aircraft, and while the base was being built, 400 miles of unexplored coastline were photographed from the air.

The wintering party made a number of field journeys using new equipment, and their achievements threw light on many of the scientific problems to be tackled by their successors. In later years a second continental base, Davis, was set up. In addition to valuable meteorological and geophysical work, major exploratory journeys from both stations resulted in the mapping and geological examination of a number of newly discovered mountain ranges. The bases, established largely as the result of political pressures, fully justified themselves as valuable centres for scientific research.

With the advent of the International Geophysical Year (*see chap. 11*) Australasia came into its own. Not only did Australia increase her activities in line with the needs of IGY programmes, but New Zealand took the opportunity to begin research in her Ross Dependency. As a first step a geophysical team of five was attached to the Ross Sea Party of the Trans-Antarctic Expedition (*see chap. 12*). On the conclusion of the expedition in 1958 the New Zealand government decided to continue the scientific work, and Scott Base in McMurdo Sound has been maintained ever since.

Through the years New Zealand scientists have made substantial contributions in geology, glaciology, geophysics and marine biology. It was fortunate that the invitations to participate in the TAE and the IGY were coincident. Had it been otherwise, the New Zealand government might not have found itself in possession of an established base, experienced men, and an on-going scientific programme. The existence of all these was persuasive, and New Zealand rightly takes pride in her Antarctic possessions and all that is being achieved there.

9
American Exploration

American interest in the Antarctic dates from 1839 when the disastrous United States Exploring Expedition, consisting of six ships under the command of Lieutenant Charles Wilkes, was sent to examine the region where the South Magnetic Pole was thought to be. The men were inadequately clothed, the ships were in poor condition, and their commander sailed feeling that he was 'doomed to destruction'. Only three vessels reached the Antarctic, and were then separated by gales, the men suffering great hardship. Though land was reported almost daily, subsequent exploration disproved its existence; the crews must have seen only distant ice masses frozen into the pack. On his return Wilkes was court-martialled, accused of injustice and oppression, and of having faked his discoveries. United States interest then lapsed until 1928.

In that year British, Norwegian, German and American expeditions were in the field, and it was an Australian, Sir Hubert Wilkins, who introduced the first aircraft into the Antarctic. He had flown the early military planes, and was convinced that they could revolutionize polar exploration. Sponsored by the American Geographical Society and backed by the Hearst press, the Wilkins-Hearst Flight arrived at Deception Island. It consisted of two Lockheed Vegas equipped to land on wheels, skis or floats. The intention was to fly some 600 miles to an advance base at the head of the Graham Land peninsula, and there refuel for a 2000-mile flight across unexplored territory to the Bay of Whales.

The first test flight, made by the co-pilot Ben Eielson, was on 16 November, and ten days later both aircraft took off on a round flight of nearly 1300 miles in an unsuccessful attempt to find an 'aerodrome' further south. The mountainous peninsula offered no suitable landing strips, but from the air both pilots were convinced that Graham Land was in fact a series of islands separated by narrow ice-filled channels. It was not until 1935 that this was disproved by the British Graham Land Expedition under John Rymill. As a result of their flights and sledge journeys, it was established that the supposed 'channels' were glaciers flowing down both sides of the razor-backed peninsula.

In the same year an American, Lincoln Ellsworth, and Herbert Hollick-Kenyon, an English pilot flying for Canadian Airways, carried out Wilkins's original project. Having established a forward air base on Dundee Island, their first attempt to fly across to the Bay of Whales was frustrated by mechanical failure. A second flight next day reached a point further south than Wilkins had achieved before a blizzard forced them to turn back. On 23 November they set out for the third time in perfect weather. They flew over a whole new region, and to within 16 miles of the Bay of Whales before their fuel ran out and the plane had to be abandoned. The men marched to the coast where a ship was sent to evacuate them.

The man who dominated American Antarctic activities for thirty years was a naval officer, Richard Byrd, who in 1928 commanded a United States expedition to the Bay of Whales. Like Amundsen, he decided to establish a base on the shelf ice. Two ships, the *City of New York* and *Eleanor Bolling*, carried three ski-equipped monoplanes, 100 dogs and 665 tons of cargo. The first large-scale modern expedition had arrived.

Their base, Little America, consisted of three main huts, linked by parallel walls built from the packing cases which contained the stores, and roofed over. As the snow drifted over the whole complex the station was slowly buried, but the stores were easily accessible in the passageways. For the first time, electric light and telephones were installed, and tall radio masts kept the men in daily contact with the world outside.

Within three weeks of their arrival, inland flights began. Aerial cameras photographed coasts and mountain chains which would have taken months of dog-sledging to discover. Sometimes new land was seen at the rate of 4000 square miles per hour.

There were a number of research projects. One was a geological journey led by Dr Laurence Gould to examine the mountains of the Queen Maud Range, lying across the route up to the polar plateau. Another was the first flight over the South Pole. Gould's party sledged into the foothills of the mountains, from where they could report when weather conditions were suitable for the flight, and also provide a rescue team should anything go wrong. As soon as they were in position, Byrd with three companions took off in a tri-motored Ford from Little America.

When loaded with sufficient fuel to cover the distance, the plane had a ceiling of barely 11,000 feet. This gave a margin of only 500 feet to clear the range, and at one stage of the flight only the ejection of food bags enabled the plane to regain sufficient buoyancy to 'creep over the hump'. But Byrd reached the Pole, over which a United States flag was thrown out, and the Ford turned back, landing safely after nineteen hours in the air.

The geological party worked their way eastwards along the foot of the Queen Maud Range, discovering a number of the glaciers which flow down into the Ross Ice Shelf. The United States recognised no national territorial sectors, but when the party reached a new region it was named Marie Byrd Land and unofficially 'claimed'.

In 1933 Byrd returned to Little America. The station had disappeared under the ice, but eight new huts were erected on the site and became Little America II. Nothing was then known about winter weather conditions inland, though it was clear that the great torrents of cold air which pour off the plateau must have a considerable effect on atmospheric circulation. To study this, Byrd planned to set up a meteorological station, manned by four people, as far inland as possible.

In March the first mechanised convoy, consisting of three light Citroen vans mounted on tracks and a six-ton Cletrac tractor, set off. In case the Cletrac fell into a crevasse, the controls were attached to 60-foot ropes and it was 'driven' by a man on foot, but after 67 miles it broke down and was abandoned. Advance Base was finally established 123 miles inland. In an effort to avoid the problem of snow drifts, a small pre-fabricated hut was lowered into a pit dug in the ice so that the ceiling was flush with the surface. A trap-door in the roof led out of the building. Food had been abandoned with the Cletrac, and as a result it was impossible to support four men through the winter. Rather than risk the nervous tensions which Byrd thought might arise between two men, he decided to man the station alone. When all the equipment had been set up, the support party returned to Little America.

Six weeks after they left, Byrd began feeling dizzy. He found that cracks in the joints of the stove pipe were allowing oil fumes to leak into the tiny hut and the ventilators were clogged with drift. As best he could, he filled in the cracks, and constantly cleared the vents. Three times a week he spoke to Little America, the base transmitting in voice while he replied in morse. During a radio 'sched' in May, the petrol generator which powered his equipment failed. Suddenly the snow tunnel, where the engine was still running, filled with fumes. Telling base to wait, he rushed to adjust a valve, and within moments he fell down unconscious. But the air on the floor of the tunnel was still pure and he quickly recovered sufficiently to stagger back to the radio and sign off.

On his hands and knees he crawled back into the tunnel and turned off the engine, but he was suffering from carbon-monoxide poisoning, and for the rest of the winter he never recovered. For weeks he lay in his sleeping bag, suffering headaches and excruciating pain in his limbs. It was a terrible struggle to cope even with the daily chores, but somehow he also forced himself to climb the ladder to the surface each day to read the meteorological instruments. Frightened of more trouble with his stove, he formed the habit of letting it out for three or four hours each day, often eating his food half frozen.

June was a ghastly month, and in July the temperature at Advance Base dropped to −80°F. Finally the motor generator broke down completely, and radio communication had to be maintained by an emergency hand-cranked

19. *Admiral Richard Byrd* USN

machine. His strength was insufficient to keep up the cranking. After every few words he had to ask base to wait, and after every sched he was played out for many hours. At last his messages became so confused that the men at Little America realised that something must be seriously wrong, and in the depths of winter a tractor party set out for Advance Base. Twice weather conditions and mechanical failures drove them back, but on 8 August a third attempt succeeded. When the relief party arrived they were deeply shocked at the weakness and gaunt appearance of their leader. For two months they nursed him back to health, and by then it was summer. An aircraft flew in from Little America and Advance Base was closed down. Despite Byrd's very serious illness, a complete set of meteorological records was brought out.

In the following summer many more long flights criss-crossed the interior producing photographic records of new areas, and much geological work was done by tractor parties travelling thousands of miles. Low-grade coal seams were found in a number of sites. Fragments of fossilized tree trunks 12 to 18 inches thick were brought back, and at an altitude of 5000 feet lichens were seen growing on exposed rock which faced the sun and was sheltered from the wind. It was a very fruitful expedition, and of the men who went south with Byrd, Richard Black, Richard Cruzen, George Dufek, Finn Ronne and Dr Paul Siple later all became leaders in their own right.

By 1939 political rivalry was growing and, as in the case of Australia, the United States government determined that she must not be left out of any future development of this vast empty continent. The US Antarctic Service was established under Admiral Byrd, and a series of long-term expeditions was initiated. Their primary aim was the exploration of Marie Byrd Land, the sector where a potential American claim would be strongest.

In January 1940 two ships, the *Bear* and the *North Star*, arrived in the Bay of Whales to set up 'West Base' at Little America III. Since Byrd's last visit, pressure ice had bent and crushed the old huts. A new site was chosen for a large complex of buildings, which included the main living hut, a machine shop, a science building, and large hangars where aircraft could winter under cover. The ships then sailed round to Marguerite Bay, and 'East Base' was established at Stonington Island. Byrd planned a series of flights from both stations in order to chart the 1700 miles of coastline which lay between. Dog teams and tractor trains from West Base would also explore the hinterland eastwards, while parties from East Base worked southwards to meet them.

It is not possible to give an account here of all the adventures which befell this expedition. Both groups travelled many miles and a great deal of work was accomplished. But by the time they were relieved the following year, the United States was on the brink of war. The men returned home to join the armed services, and few scientific results were ever published. The idea of setting up permanent American Antarctic stations had to be shelved.

When the Second World War ended and the United States and the Soviet Union emerged as the two great powers, their political differences were sadly apparent. The shortest distance between them lies straight across the Arctic basin. It was therefore argued that American servicemen should be trained in polar techniques, and military equipment be tested under polar conditions. This, plus the government's policy of maintaining a foothold in Antarctica, led to the organisation of Operation Highjump, a summer expedition to Little America.

This was an entirely new conception, and the largest single exploratory expedition ever mounted. For the first time, ordinary cargo ships, carrying a variety of vehicles, aircraft and seaplanes, followed modern icebreakers into the Ross Sea, while ski-equipped aircraft flew in from a naval carrier which lay outside the pack ice. Thirteen ships and 4700 men took part, with Admiral Byrd in overall command, and Admiral Cruzen in command of the Task Force. The ships were divided into three flotillas, which attempted to penetrate the ice in different places. The flagship of the central group was the icebreaker *Northwind*.

It turned out to be an exceptionally bad ice season. Belts of pack stretched for 600 miles, and the ships were constantly in collision with it. The *Northwind* dashed about like an anxious collie herding sheep, breaking out ship after ship, desperately trying to keep a channel open and the convoy moving. Aircraft were called in to reconnoitre the ice ahead, while slowly the ships fought through to the site of Little America IV.

This was a tented camp, established some two miles from the 1940 site. An airstrip 5000 feet long and 150 feet wide was laid out, complete with runway lights. Meanwhile, the aircraft carrier *Philippine Sea* prepared to launch her planes from outside the pack. On 29 January 1947 her six twin-engined Douglas transports (DC3s) began flying in. It was the first time heavy ski-equipped planes had been launched from a carrier. Once airborne they *had* to reach their destination, for their great wing spread made it impossible for them to land-on again.

The scientific programme ranged from examination of the sea bottom to studies of the ionosphere. It was clear that the Bay of Whales was shrinking, the two sides being slowly pressed together, and studies of the Ross Ice Shelf were begun. But the major project was a number of exploratory flights deep into the hinterland. For these, every moment of clear weather was used, the pilots making do with the minimum of sleep, while ground crews worked round the clock to keep the planes serviced. Motorised convoys carrying aviation fuel travelled into the interior to establish weather stations and emergency landing strips, while the flights fanned out in all directions. In the course of

64 sorties photographs were taken covering areas estimated at more than 350,000 square miles. Eighteen new mountain ranges were discovered with peaks averaging 15 to 20,000 feet and by the time the ships sailed home only one major stretch of coast had still never been seen – that south of the Weddell Sea.

The following season, 1947/8, a new expedition, Operation Windmill, used helicopters based on icebreakers to land on inaccessible parts of the coast. During these operations there were many mishaps and close shaves, for a helicopter's range is very limited and they are much more vulnerable in bad weather than ordinary aircraft. However, they provide a means whereby scientists can be lifted to places which cannot be reached in any other way, and have since become a normal part of American Antarctic transport.

10
The British Sector

The first title to Antarctic territories was established in 1908 when the British government formally claimed the sector of Antarctica which lies to the south of South America and converges on the Pole. All these lands (South Georgia, South Sandwich Islands, South Shetland Islands, South Orkney Islands and Graham Land) had first been discovered by British explorers. They now became Dependencies of the Falkland Islands, under the jurisdiction of the Governor. British claims to the Ross Dependency and Australian Antarctic Territory were made in 1923 and 1933 respectively, and these areas were later transferred to the jurisdiction of New Zealand and Australia.

At the beginning of the century, a number of Norwegian, Chilean and British whaling companies were licensed to hunt whales in the Falkland Islands Dependencies. The cold Antarctic waters are very prolific. Besides large numbers of whales, there are quantities of sponges, corals, worms, star fish, sea anemones, sea cucumbers, and sea spiders with ten legs. Small one-celled plants called diatoms provide food for the tiniest marine animals, the foraminifera and infusoria. Shrimps, krill and other small crustaceans live on the infusoria, while fish, penguins and seals feed on the crustaceans. Fish and penguins in turn become the food of the sea leopards. But it is the whale which is the most important animal commercially.

For centuries there had been a profitable whaling industry in the Arctic, mainly in the waters around Iceland and Greenland where the sperm whale flourished. Whale oil was the basis for wax candles, cooking fats, soap and cosmetics. In the reign of Victoria, when ladies of fashion achieved their tiny waists by wearing tight corsets 'stayed' with whalebone, the market price reached £3000 per ton. The capture of a single whale then defrayed the cost of an entire voyage, and English, Dutch, Scandinavian and American fleets finally destroyed the Arctic stocks.

In 1892 the first Scottish and Norwegian whalers turned to the south, where they soon realised that the more aggressive species found in the Antarctic waters were more difficult to handle than the northern sperm whales. The story is told of one whaler in the Weddell Sea, which managed to get three harpoons into a finback and was at once carried off by the whale. As it rushed past, a second boat got three more lines into it. But still the whale tore through the water, towing the boats and 720 fathoms of cable. A third boat joined the battle, and succeeded in carrying the free ends of all the lines back to the mother ship. But the whale now towed the ship and the three boats, and at the end of 14 hours it was still pulling strongly. In a final bid to halt it the ship's engines were put into reverse. This snapped the cables, the whale disappeared and the whalers lost their equipment.

When the whaling companies were first licensed, it was necessary to bring the whales ashore for processing and it was thus possible to control the numbers killed. All the companies paid dues to the Falkland Islands government, and it was forbidden to kill a whale calf, or a female still accompanied by her calf. But by the mid-twenties, many whaling companies began to install processing plant and haul-up slipways in huge factory ships. When these put to sea, whales could be hunted indiscriminately anywhere on the oceans. By 1930 over-production had so reduced the price of oil that it became necessary to try to arrive at some kind of international agreement.

The Discovery Committee, set up in London in 1923 to investigate the biology of the southern oceans, also began studies of the different whale populations. It was hoped that this would make it easier to regulate their hunting in the best interests of the industry. British scientists established a Marine Biological Station at Grytviken in South Georgia, where every whale brought ashore from the catchers was examined before it was processed. Much was learnt about their age, rate of growth, breeding habits and diseases. The investigators also wanted to learn about their environment – the waters in which they lived, their food requirements and so on. For this purpose Scott's *Discovery* was fitted out as an oceanographic vessel.

She arrived in South Georgia in 1926, and a year later was joined by the *William Scoresby* which played a large part in the systematic marking of whales. Dated barbs were fired into their blubber, and when later an animal was recovered at the whaling station, these gave useful information on whale migration.

Throughout many cruises in Dependency waters, the two vessels occupied a large number of scientific stations. This entailed a ship being hove-to for about three hours while her exact position was plotted and a number of simultaneous observations made. These included the temperature and salinity of the sea at various depths, soundings, observations on the distribution of plankton, and the dredging of samples from the ocean bottom. Thus a picture of oceanic conditions was gradually built up.

The *Discovery* was the first Antarctic ship able to receive the Greenwich time signal, and at last it was possible to plot accurate longitudes. It was then found that of all the lands mapped around Graham Land and the South Shetlands, only Deception Island had been charted in its correct position.

This scientific work, known as the Discovery Investigations, lasted for 12 years, until the ships were withdrawn at the outbreak of the Second World

20. Early whalers

War. They produced a wealth of data, and provided useful information to the international whaling conferences, which were trying to regulate the industry and protect the stocks. But constant commercial pressures on governments prevented them from agreeing to effective controls, so the whale populations were dangerously reduced. Today all shore-based whaling has ceased. Japanese and Russian factory ships continue to operate at sea, but it will soon become an unprofitable venture.

As the number of whales has decreased, so the krill on which they feed has been able to multiply. Today scientists are considering whether it is better for man to harvest krill for its fat and protein, or leave it so that the whale stocks may build up again.

In 1925 Argentina laid claim to Graham Land. The claim was based on geographical proximity and the fact that the old papal decree of the fifteenth century had given all new lands discovered in the western hemisphere to Spain. Argentina argued that she had inherited this Spanish right. In 1940 the Chilean government also put forward a claim to Graham Land, based not only on geographical proximity, but on the grounds that geologically the peninsula is a continuation of the Andes. The situation developed into a bitter political dispute, but both countries refused Britain's offer to submit the case for arbitration to the International Court of Justice.

By 1943 it was realised that despite the war, more obvious steps must be

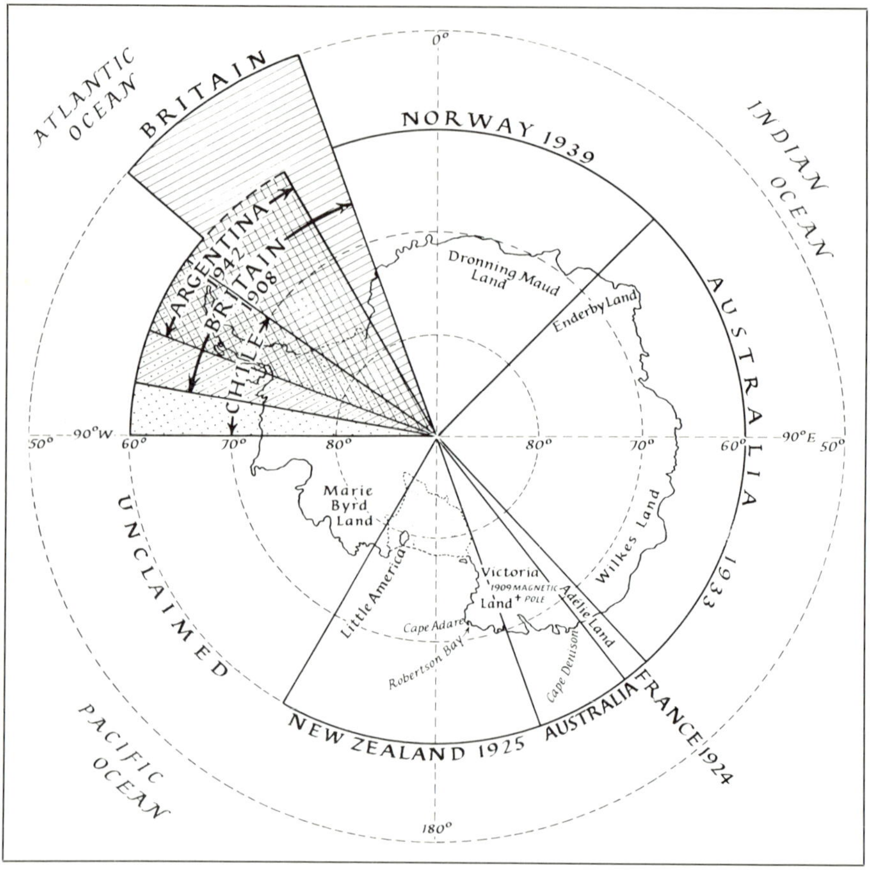

Map 4. National claims in Antarctica

taken to occupy the British-claimed sector of Antarctica, and under the code name Operation Tabarin a small expedition was organised. In the first season, bases were established at Deception Island and Port Lockroy on Wiencke Island. The two Base Commanders were sworn in as magistrates by the Governor of the Falkland Islands, and charged with the administration of the area under their control. Each base was a recognised post office, and Falkland Islands stamps were used for letters home.

Although the stations were occupied for political reasons, they provided platforms for scientific work, and useful projects were immediately set in train. Each base had a radio transmitter, and throughout the year twice-daily weather reports were passed to Stanley in the Falkland Islands. At Port Lockroy, where mosses and lichens are to be found, botanical as well as marine

21. *'Dog teams were taken south . . .'*

zoological collections were made. In the following season a third base opened at Hope Bay and dog teams were taken south. It then became possible for surveyors and geologists to make long journeys, mapping the region and studying the structure of the rocks. So began the first continuous Antarctic expedition, which is still in progress today. When the Second World War ended its name was changed to the Falkland Islands Dependencies Survey (FIDS).

By 1948, there were seven FIDS bases, under the overall command of Dr Vivian Fuchs who had his headquarters at Stonington Island. Lessons learnt from the experiences of the early pioneers had resulted in improved rations and clothing, but above all dog teams had now become the normal means of travel at British stations. Originally imported from Labrador, huskies were bred at the bases, and often during a single summer the journeys from one station alone would cover 15,000 to 20,000 miles. These hardy and hard-working animals had come into their own. The men came to believe that they could manage and drive them better even than the Eskimoes.

As the continuous scientific work began to produce more and more interesting results, the political overtones often produced situations akin to farce. Argentina and Chile established bases in the disputed sector, sometimes within a hundred yards of a British station. Geographical features already well known by existing names were arbitrarily re-named, leading to confusion in international publications. As the relief ships arrived each season, the various Base Commanders were compelled to call upon the captains to deliver Notes of Protest on behalf of their governments, complaining at this infringement of territorial waters without permission. But as soon as the awkward formalities were concluded, everyone would be welcomed on board or at the base for a party.

While the politicians wrangled, and in most areas the men in the field unofficially maintained friendly relations, the *Times* was pleading for common sense:

> . . . national jealousy should not be allowed to find a field in the one continent where it has hitherto been lacking . . . Antarctica is not a fit subject for national rivalries or political bargaining. Its future, if in doubt, should be decided by law in the interests of science.

When the Falklands War erupted in 1982 there was a fear that hostilities would extend to Antarctica, but happily this did not happen.

THE AGE OF SCIENTIFIC CO-OPERATION

11

The International Geophysical Year

It was an Austrian naval officer and explorer, Lieutenant Karl Weyprecht, who first suggested that scientific results would be of much greater value if nations organised their polar expeditions simultaneously and pooled their data. As a result, the first International Polar Year took place in 1882–3, and a second one 50 years later. The studies of geophysical phenomena revealed that the number of sun spots and particles emitted by the sun varies throughout an 11-year cycle. Twenty-five years after this, in order to study the interaction of the sun with the Earth's atmosphere at a period of maximum sun spot activity, a special international committee was set up in Paris to organise the International Geophysical Year (IGY) of 1957–8.

Sixty-six nations took part in these simultaneous observations all over the world, and 12 countries undertook to establish stations in the Antarctic. (These countries were: Argentina, Australia, Belgium, Chile, France, Japan, New Zealand, Norway, South Africa, the Soviet Union, the United Kingdom and the United States.) The scientific programmes were co-ordinated and measuring procedures standardized, to ensure that data collected by one nation could be compared with that from others.

Altogether 44 Antarctic stations were set up. Britain already had ten FIDS bases in the region of the Antarctic Peninsula. In addition, the Royal Society established a larger and more sophisticated geophysical observatory at Halley Bay. Built on a floating ice shelf some 500 feet thick, the position of the station was found to be in an area of maximum auroral activity. This was fortunate for it ensured the best results in ionospheric and other upper atmosphere studies.

The Soviet Union put in five stations and two staging bases, and succeeded in the difficult task of establishing Sovetskaya at the point on the continent furthest away from any coast – the Pole of Relative Inaccessibility. Tractors hauled the material 1300 miles from their coastal station at Mirny.

The largest national contribution was organised by the Americans under the name 'Operation Deepfreeze'. This involved nearly 5000 men, four ice-breakers, cargo ships and numerous aircraft. A large Antarctic 'township', complete with an airfield on the sea ice, was set up at McMurdo Sound. Here the ships landed thousands of tons of material, which was then carried by tractor trains or aircraft to establish five other stations, some of them deep

Map 5. Stations occupied during the IGY

in the hinterland. Amundsen/Scott, at the South Pole itself, was established and is still maintained entirely by air. Apart from the smaller aircraft brought south in the ships, huge Globemasters flew in regularly from New Zealand, while tankers were frozen in for the winter to provide fuel for the operations.

The principal objectives of the IGY were the examination of the Earth and its atmosphere, and the effect of the sun upon them. To accomplish this, studies were made of aurorae, cosmic rays, geomagnetism, glaciology, ionospheric physics, meteorology, seismology and gravity. Many nations also included biology, geology, and oceanographic work.

It was recognised that the observations of the greatest practical value would be comprehensive meteorological records for a better understanding of world weather systems, and all bases co-operated in this work. Each day a network of 39 'daughter' stations relayed their three-hourly observations to eight 'mother' stations, from which the information was transmitted to the IGY Weather Central at Little America V. Here a team of meteorologists from six countries drew the upper air and surface charts, and prepared weather forecasts which were issued daily. For the first time, an overall and comprehensive picture of Antarctic weather conditions began to emerge.

This great experiment in joint scientific endeavour was so successful, and produced such a wealth of information, that the activities were extended for a further year of International Geophysical Co-operation (IGC). Then in 1964–5, when sun spot activity was at its minimum, another world wide co-operative effort was initiated called the International Years of the Quiet Sun (IQSY), when again a comparative series of observations were made, in which all the Antarctic stations played their part.

From the IGY, it was clear that the great scientific gains in Antarctica had been possible only because the political problems had been put on one side. Formal approaches were then made to convene an international conference, to be attended by representatives of the 12 nations working there. Its purpose was to discuss the solution of their political differences, and to arrange some kind of 'internationalization' of the continent. A series of conferences began in Washington in 1959 and in 1961 an Antarctic Treaty was signed which is to be reviewed in 1991.

The Treaty covers the area south of latitude 60°S. It recognises

> . . . that it is in the interests of all mankind that Antarctica shall continue for ever to be used exclusively for peaceful purposes and shall not become the scene or object of international discord.

Under its terms the establishment of military bases, the testing of weapons, nuclear explosions, or the disposal of radioactive waste material is forbidden. All national territorial claims are in abeyance or 'frozen', and every part of the continent is open to the scientists of any nation. The British sector lying within the Treaty area is now called British Antarctic Territory, and only South Georgia and the South Sandwich Islands remain as the Falkland Islands Dependencies. In addition, the Falkland Islands Dependencies Survey has been re-named the British Antarctic Survey.

Since the signing of this Treaty, scientific co-operation has been intensified and a tradition of real friendship is being built up. Each nation supplies details of all the facilities available at their bases, whether occupied or closed, and publishes what has been left in field huts or depots. Thus ground parties, or aircraft crews which may get into trouble, know exactly where food, fuel or aviation spirit can be obtained, where emergency landings can be made, what medical facilities can be expected, and so on.

All scientific results are freely exchanged and joint programmes are constantly organised. For seven years Hallett, in Victoria Land, was shared by

22. Upper air balloon release by Australians at Wilkes Station

New Zealanders and Americans. In 1959 the United States handed over to Australia their station in Wilkes Land; a well-established base for 17 men, and a million pounds' worth of equipment. At a short, moving ceremony, a new set of scientists took over and work continued without pause. For three years the Americans and Argentinians shared Ellsworth. Belgium and Holland set up a joint base in Dronning Maud Land in 1964, while the Russians at Vostok operated American equipment as part of a cosmic ray study being carried out by scientists in the States. A British glaciologist has wintered at Mirny in exchange for a Russian geologist at Stonington, and a British biologist lived for a year with the Argentinians at Almirante Brown. These are but a few examples of the co-operative spirit which has been achieved.

Three World Data Centres (WDCS) have been agreed upon where all the information is deposited. One is in the United States, the second in the Soviet Union, and the third is dispersed between scientific institutions all over the world. These Centres are concerned with particular sciences, and each sends copies of all the material it receives to the other two.

The Treaty now operates on two levels, political and scientific. The Scientific Committee on Antarctic Research (SCAR), where all the Treaty nations are represented, is responsible for the formulation and co-ordination of a broad programme of scientific investigation. Its secretariat is at the Scott Polar Research Institute, Cambridge. Within it are established Working Groups to co-ordinate activities in each science, and meetings are held every two years in different host countries.

At government level, Consultative Meetings are held periodically, when representatives of the contracting parties exchange information and make recommendations to their governments for the furtherance of the objectives of the Treaty. One outstanding achievement has been the adoption of 'Agreed Measures for the Conservation of Antarctic Flora and Fauna'.

The Antarctic offers unique research opportunities to biologists, for the environment has not been interfered with by man. This was recognised by SCAR, which brought to the attention of the Treaty Powers the need to establish rules which all expeditions should observe in relation to animals and plants. Now there are 'Specially Protected Species', and 'Specially Protected Areas' which cover such places as breeding grounds and plant communities.

For scientific investigation, and also to feed dog teams, it is necessary each year to kill or capture a number of seals. This can be done only under a properly controlled permit system, and each nation is required to report and justify the numbers taken. Fur seals may not be touched at all.

The whole of Antarctica is thus subject to the most modern principles of wild life conservation. The Treaty has brought enormous benefits to the area covered by its terms, and it has been suggested that it should be used as a prototype for the negotiation of a 'Space Treaty' to regulate the behaviour of men who may soon be living on the Moon.

12
The Commonwealth Trans-Antarctic Expedition

While in command of the FIDS bases in 1949, Dr Vivian Fuchs, with one companion, made a geological dog-sledge journey of 1080 miles from Stonington. Lying tent-bound for four days during a blizzard, he began to plan a crossing of the continent from the Weddell Sea to the Ross Sea, a distance of some 2000 miles. Among other things he wanted to find out what lay under the ice cap, and to discover whether Antarctica is one large landmass, or whether it consists of two or more great islands divided by a strait, joined together only by the ice sheet.

Originally conceived as an independent and entirely self-supporting venture, it took six years to obtain support from four Commonwealth governments (the United Kingdom, New Zealand, Australia, and South Africa), and sufficient backing from industry. By then the IGY was being organised and the expedition played its part in the scientific programmes. Fuchs intended to put the crossing party ashore in Vahsel Bay. To support it on the final stages of the journey, a New Zealand group under Sir Edmund Hillary was to establish a reception base in McMurdo Sound, and then lay a series of depots for 700 miles towards the Pole.

On 14 November 1955 the expedition sailed from London in the *Theron*. The little ship could hardly be seen for the mountain of stores she carried. Her deck space was entirely filled by two huge crates containing a Sno-Cat and an Auster aircraft, and a hundred barrels of fuel. On top of these were kennels for the 24 Greenland huskies, small boats, lengths of piping, building materials, and hundreds of items which could not be fitted into her bulging holds.

The *Theron* was only the second ship to enter the Weddell Sea since the *Endurance* was crushed 40 years earlier. She in turn was beset for 33 days, but reached Vahsel Bay on 29 January 1956. The season was already well advanced and the men worked round the clock to unload the stores before the sea froze over and trapped the ship. Shackleton Base was established on the Filchner Ice Shelf, one mile from the edge of the ice cliffs. The expedition then sailed for home to collect more material and scientific equipment for the crossing, leaving behind an advance party of eight under K. V. Blaiklock. Their task was to build the base to which the main party would return the following season.

23. *Building the hut at Shackleton*

At the beginning of March the weather deteriorated. Blinding drift obliterated everything, and strong winds broke up the sea ice on which a large amount of stores still remained stacked. When the blizzard was over, the men found only open water – all their coal and much of their food and fuel had disappeared. As a result the advance party spent perhaps the hardest winter endured by anyone since Scott's Northern Party at the beginning of the century.

They lived in the Sno-Cat crate (20 by 9 by 8 feet), and slept in two-man tents which were continually buried by drifting snow. One end of the crate was the 'radio-room', the other end the 'kitchen', where an ingenious oven was improvised from an empty oil drum. There was always an inch of ice on the floor, while condensation from the cooking, and from their breath, froze into stalactites which hung down from the ceiling. In the old days when parties got into trouble, they had no choice but to endure their hardships. But these eight men had a radio, sledging rations and fresh dogs. Belgrano, an Argentine IGY base where they could have taken refuge, was only 50 miles away. They chose to remain and, despite continual struggles against the weather, the hut was slowly built.

Meanwhile, in London and Wellington, final preparations were made for the main parties to sail south. In November 1956 Fuchs sailed from Tower Bridge in the *Magga Dan*. A month later Hillary left Wellington in HMNZS *Endeavour*, to set up Scott Base at Pram Point, in McMurdo Sound. The *Magga Dan* was shared with the Royal Society party who were going to occupy Halley Bay, which lay 200 miles north of Shackleton. The station was Britain's main contribution to the IGY, after which it was taken over as a FIDS base.

On 13 January 1957 Shackleton Base was relieved, and the hard pressed advance party received their first mail for a year. Now all energies were directed to finding a suitable site for a small inland station 300 miles towards the Pole.

This advance base was named South Ice. It was established entirely by air, a single-engined Otter making 20 flights, carrying one ton of material at a time. A small prefabricated hut was built in a specially dug pit where it quickly became buried, the snow providing good insulation against the winter temperatures which fell to −76°F. For seven months three men lived there, carrying out glaciological studies and maintaining four-hourly meteorological observations. The base finally became the last depot through which the crossing party passed on their way to the Pole.

At all three Trans-Antarctic Expedition (TAE) stations winter was a busy time, both for the scientists who were taking part in the IGY programmes, and the engineers who were preparing the tractors for their challenging journey. When the sun returned, field parties with dog teams were flown out to examine newly discovered mountain areas, and particularly the Shackleton Range which was first seen during the flights to South Ice.

At the same time, the New Zealanders set out from Scott Base to lay depots towards the Pole. With dog teams and two modified Ferguson farm tractors, the ground party found suitable vehicle routes and chose the sites. Their Beaver aircraft then flew in the supplies to establish the depots.

Fuchs himself led the route-finding reconnaissance journey to South Ice. Four tractors, at times roped together like mountaineers, set out on what proved to be the most nerve-racking experience. Huge crevassed areas had to be crossed, and with heartbreaking regularity the fragile snow bridges collapsed under the weight of vehicles. Deep chasms opened up and tractors fell in, each time posing a new problem of how they could be extricated. The recoveries were dangerous, highly skilled operations, and it was often five or six hours before a vehicle was safely back on the surface.

The men soon invented a technique of probing the way ahead on skis. Every yard a long aluminium pole was plunged into the ground to its full length. If it broke through the surface, the crevasse beneath was opened up and examined – sometimes by a man climbing down into it. By discovering the direction in which it ran, it was possible to flag a safe passage through to the next

24. A narrow escape

one. Laboriously they marked out a tortuous path, and Fuchs' journal reflected his anxiety:

> ... the next ten miles are going to make or break the expedition for we may lose vehicles ... With crash helmets, safety straps and roped vehicles we have taken all the precautions we can.

It took 37 days to reach South Ice. Leaving the tractors there, they flew back to Shackleton in two and a half hours, and nine days later they started all over again.

On 24 November 1957 the trans-continental journey began. Each vehicle hauled two sledges, and the trek to South Ice was a sorry repetition of their first experience. Their highest speed when roped together was 3½ mph and for hours on end they drove at 1 mph in bottom gear – nicknamed 'Grandma'. The warmer summer temperatures had further weakened the snow bridges crossed during the reconnaissance journey. Twice in one day Ken Blaiklock

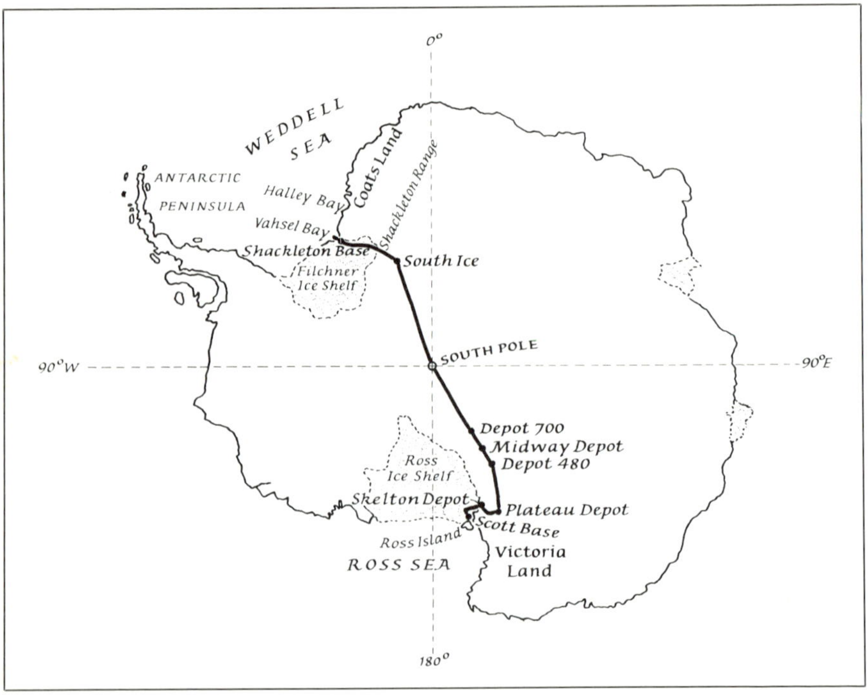

Map 6. TAE *route across Antarctica*

nearly perished. First a snow bridge gave way exactly where he stood and his skis, which he had deftly stepped out of, fell 80 feet into the hole. A few hours later he was kneeling on new skis peering into a crevasse when suddenly the bridge under him fell away. Each end of the skis remained supported, with Ken kneeling in the middle over a gap four feet wide. Later, as Jon Stephenson, the geologist, walked to his tent the snow gave way and left him hanging by one elbow over a dark cavern which appeared to be bottomless. Often whole areas had to be probed all over again; Fuchs wrote in his diary:

> . . . the last mile was the worst, but the tortuous course was gay with coloured flags, stakes and ski sticks – 98 of them in one mile, each marking a particularly hazardous point, for minor crevasses we now crossed without concern. In the bright sunlight the scene was suggestive of a course prepared for some nightmare 'bending race'.

With worn nerves, but with all the tractors intact, they reached South Ice on 21 December. They remained there four days, overhauling the battered vehicles and re-stowing the sledges for the longest leg of the journey – 550 miles to the Pole, and then another 500 miles to their first supply dump at Depot 700.

On the other side of the continent the New Zealanders had made unexpectedly fast progress in good weather conditions. By 20 December all the depots were laid, and it was clear that it would be some time before the two groups met. Hillary decided on a quick dash to the Pole 'for the Hell of it'. His farm tractors had done much more than had been expected in getting to Depot 700. But now the soft surfaces and high altitude proved almost too much for them. The party jettisoned every unnecessary ounce, and with much coaxing from devoted mechanics, the Fergusons struggled to Amundsen/Scott Station (the American IGY base at the South Pole) on 4 January 1958 – the first party to arrive there overland since Scott himself.

The crossing party left South Ice on Christmas Day. Two dog teams ran ahead to reconnoitre the route, and as part of an enormous load of equipment, the tractors carried 21 tons of fuel and half a ton of explosives for the seismic work. In order to discover the depths of ice on the polar plateau a 'seismic shot' was fired every 30 miles. This entailed drilling a 30-foot hole, at the bottom of which an explosive charge was fired. The shock waves from the explosion travelled through the ice, 'bouncing' back to the surface from the rock below. The time interval between the explosion and the return of the waves was recorded in the seismic Sno-Cat. Since the speed at which they travelled through the ice was known, it was possible to calculate its depth, and as a series of shots took place right across the continent, the undulations of the land beneath the ice cap were also discovered.

The dog drivers marked the route up to the plateau by building a snow cairn every 5 miles. As time went on they became ambitious and produced increasingly complicated structures. The final work of art which met the astonished eyes of the vehicle party which followed was a miniature 'Snowhenge'.

The tractors travelled at night to take advantage of harder surfaces when temperatures were lowest. At one point they found themselves in an enormous field of sastrugi, where for 65 miles each driver had to judge the best course for his own vehicle. Soon they were scattered a mile or two apart, working and weaving their way among hard ridges four to five feet high. Sno-Cats were driven at less than half a mile an hour over vertical drops. Climbing to the top of a sharp-tongued ridge, they would tilt up and up, then suddenly dip violently forward, followed by the plunging sledges, completely out of control.

Every 200 miles the party stopped to service the vehicles, and always the scientific work continued. Each evening two to three hours were spent in drilling the pit for the seismic shot. The core which came from it was laid along the surface, and by examining the density of the ice, Hal Lister, the glaciologist, was able to determine how long the different layers had been in existence. Thus he could calculate how much snow had fallen on the ice cap in any

25. *Firing a seismic shot*

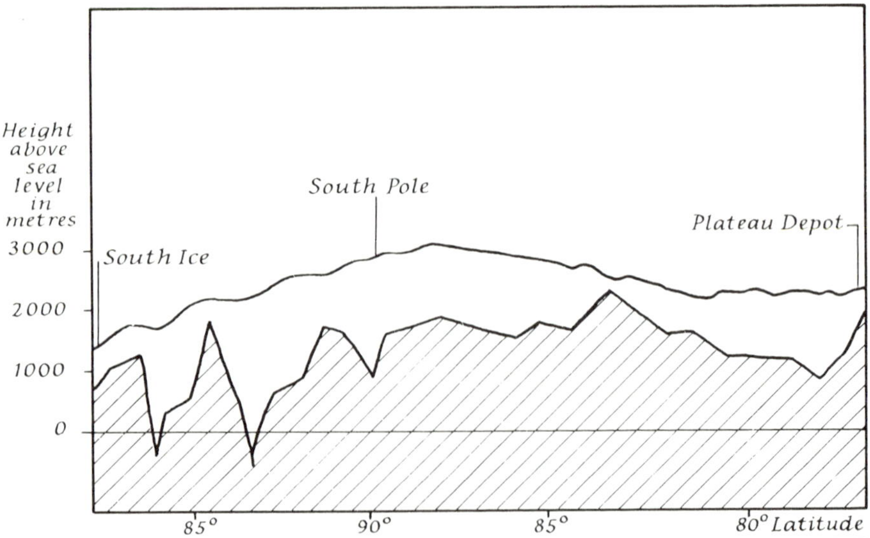

Profile of land beneath the ice sheet

given year. Thermometers were left at different depths in the pit all night. From the temperatures recorded at the various levels it was possible to calculate how much of the sun's heat penetrates into the ice cap, and what effect it has on ice crystallization.

The next morning a bell rang, warning everyone to switch off engines and remain utterly still while the seismic shot was fired. Then the cavalcade moved off, stopping at regular intervals to make gravity measurements, to take 'rammsonde' soundings, and to record the meteorological observations. The gravity measurements varied according to the amount of snow lying on top of the rock, and so filled in the gaps between the seismic shots in obtaining a profile of the land lying under the ice. The rammsonde was a complicated measuring device whereby a rod with a steel cone at the end of it was hammered down to a given depth of snow by a block of known weight dropped from a known height. The number of blows taken to reach a particular depth gave the density of the snow at that point. All this work, which included measurements of the sun's radiation, contributed to an understanding of the structure and behaviour of the great Antarctic ice sheet.

On 6 January the tractor party caught up with the dogs. After that the teams ran with the vehicles, four of which were abandoned at pre-determined intervals as the fuel and supplies they carried were used up. The dogs began to feel the strain of maintaining an average of 20 miles each day at high altitude, but on 19 January 1958 their ears pricked: suddenly a cluster of huts and radio masts had come into view. It was the South Pole station.

In contrast to Scott's heartbreaking words when he reached this 'awful place', Fuchs wrote:

> The dogs were tiring, and the convoy moved slowly so that they could keep up and arrive together with the vehicles. The day was a brilliant one, without a cloud, and only a light wind . . . As the party moved towards the Pole, I looked back and thought our convoy a brave sight; the orange 'Cats' and Weasel, together with the loaded sledges, bearing many fluttering flags of different colours . . . the great condensation plumes streamed away from the high open exhausts of the Sno-Cats . . . As we approached nearer we could see quite a crowd . . . all armed with cameras! . . . Our reception has been a most warm one and we have been invited to sleep and eat in the base instead of our tents . . .

After four days at the Pole station, during which the engineers worked round the clock to overhaul the tractors, the journey continued. Since the route had been proved by Hillary's party, dog teams were no longer required. Through the kindness of the Americans they were flown to Scott Base, where they remained to work for successive New Zealand parties which occupied the station after the expedition was over.

Without dogs, the vehicles were able to average 30 to 40 miles each day. At Depot 700 the Beaver from Scott Base brought Hillary in to join them.

As the party travelled towards the Magnetic Pole, the compasses became increasingly useless. When they had left the geographical South Pole every direction was 'north', and they had to travel for some 20 miles before stopping to take sights and decide which way 'north' they wanted to go. Since the Magnetic Pole was still 200 miles 'south' of them, according to the compass, 'east' suddenly became 'west' and *vice versa*. The nearer they got to the Magnetic Pole the more confusing it became. The sky was mostly overcast so they steered mainly by dead reckoning. They constantly encountered 'whiteout', an atmospheric condition when the light from an overcast sky is reflected on to the snow surface, back to the sky, and so on endlessly. This removes all shadows and the horizon itself. There are no landmarks and the ground disappears. It has been described as 'rather like being inside a ping-pong ball', and it is normally foolhardy to travel in such conditions.

But HMNZS *Endeavour* was waiting at Scott Base, the season was advancing, and soon she might be forced to leave for New Zealand if the sea began to freeze. Fuchs felt they must keep going at all costs. He invented a singularly uncomfortable but effective technique. Three stakes were planted along a line carefully orientated by compass. The driver of the leading Sno-Cat drove forward, while looking backwards out of the open door along the stake line, steering with his right hand behind him. His passenger provided the forward vision and controlled the accelerator pedal. As the 'Cats' began to move cautiously, a man from the leading tractor placed more and more stakes in line with the first three, thereby extending the course; while a man from the last vehicle collected them in again for use further on. The whole operation was a considerable strain, but the convoy kept moving.

So they passed on through Depot 480, Midway Depot, Plateau Depot, and reached the top of the Skelton Glacier. On 24 February they began the long, steep descent to the Ross Ice Shelf. Here they were harassed by strong 'katabatic winds' which pour down from the plateau to displace the warmer air rising from the ice shelf. These had scoured the steeper inclines so smooth and hard that the sledges slid from side to side, completely out of control. Sometimes they smashed into the rear pontoons of the towing vehicles, till they had to stop and fit heavy rope brakes under the runners to check them.

At the bottom of the glacier was their last depot. Here they carried out their final maintenance on the tractors, which the men considered to be the true heroes of the expedition. Three days later they broke camp for the last time and prepared for the run in to Scott Base.

Once more the Sno-Cats were decorated with all available flags and pennants. At Castle Rock, a fuel drum marked the start of a line of pennants, leading to a route bulldozed through the pressure ridges by the Americans from McMurdo. Soon Weasels, Ferguson tractors and even Bren-gun Carriers came streaming along the track to meet them. As the Sno-Cats thundered

26. The South Pole

and weaved between the ridges, they were escorted in front and behind by every variety of vehicle.

In front of Scott Base the party assembled on the sea ice, to be photographed from every angle. The evening before, the Americans had decided that for this unique occasion there must be a band. The Station Commander had decreed that all 'musicians' must volunteer. 'It don't matter if you can't play', he declared, 'But you gotta be able to play LOUD'. And so they did.

The first crossing of Antarctica had covered 2158 miles and had taken 99 days, one less than its leader had originally planned six years before. The engineers declared stoutly that given one week to overhaul the Sno-Cats, they would be prepared to turn round and drive all the way back!

Apart from the achievements of the main party, a number of other valuable exploratory journeys were carried out from Scott Base, and the RAF contingent led by Squadron Leader John Lewis made the first flight across Antarctica via the South Pole in a single-engined aircraft. After the crossing party had left South Ice, an auxiliary fuel tank was fitted in the Otter, which doubled its range and gave it a flying distance of 1600 miles in still air. The maximum pay-load was one ton, but the fuel alone weighed more than this. With four men dressed in bulky flying kit, plus their emergency equipment, there was anxiety as to whether the plane would even get off the ground.

In fact their first attempt failed, due to bad weather conditions, but on 6 January 1958 they tried again.

This time a following wind helped to eke out their fuel. They headed straight for the Pole, circling it several times before setting course for the Beardmore Glacier, up which the early explorers had so painfully man-hauled their sledges. From here it was 'down hill all the way' as Lewis put it. A few hours later Ross Island loomed ahead, and new friendly voices came over the air as Scott Base prepared their reception. American Navy Dakotas and Otters flew out to escort them, and as they approached the base the radio operator controlling the flight could not bear to miss the party. Shouting excitedly 'There you are! You can see the landing strip now', he abruptly went off the air and raced for the runway. In his book, *The Crossing of Antarctica*, Fuchs wrote:

> That evening, through the operators at the Pole Station, we heard that the flight had been successful. John Lewis was famous for the comment he invariably made on any kind of good news; 'Jolly good', he would say, 'Jolly good, bloody good, first class.' We were all delighted to know that they had made it and our message of congratulation was simple and direct: 'JOLLY GOOD, BLOODY GOOD, FIRST CLASS!' – and indeed it was.

During the expedition, coal seams were discovered in the Theron Mountains, though no mineral ores were found. Fossil plants taken from a number of different localities showed the rock to be over 300 million years old, and the seismic and gravity work revealed that mountain ranges lie buried in the ice cap. It was also proved that despite the different nature of the rocks in east and west Antarctica, the landmass is one continent. The physiological work included studies of the food and oxygen consumed by the men in relation to the cold they experienced and the work they did.

In 1964, the fiftieth anniversary of the epic *Endurance* expedition, Sir Vivian Fuchs speaking about the heroic era at the Scott Polar Research Institute in Cambridge said:

> The members of the 1955–58 Trans-Antarctic Expedition like to feel that Shackleton would have been happy that the project to which he had pointed the way, was in the end accomplished by a British expedition.

13
Living and Travelling

At each stage of exploration, progress has been directly linked to advances in technology. Early expeditions relied on ships for their mobility, but the old wooden sailing vessels frequently came to grief on the fringes of the pack. Modern icebreakers ensure that expeditions can reach their base sites regardless of all but the most severe ice conditions. These specially built steel ships, of immense hull strength, are usually of 3000 to 8000 tons, and carry very powerful engines driving two screws. Unlike the normal slab sides of a cargo vessel, the hull is gently rounded as this gives additional strength to resist ice pressure.

Steady progress through ice depends upon a ship's weight and power. Normally she can steam through ice up to two or three feet thick. In more severe conditions, the captain will carve a channel by charging the pack at maximum power. As the ship hits the edge, the cut-away stem enables her to rise up onto the ice and break it with her weight. In this way slow progress can be made through fields as much as 15 feet thick.

In most icebreakers 'heeling tanks' are located on either side. Many tons of water can be rapidly pumped backwards and forwards between the port and starboard tanks. This induces a roll of about five degrees each way, which is often enough to loosen the ice and set her free. The ships sometimes carry helicopters on deck for ice reconnaissance.

As soon as an expedition arrives at its base site, men become acutely aware of the problems posed by the topography and the surfaces over which they intend to travel. These vary from tide cracks in sea ice, to crevasses, sastrugi, and precipitous or rocky mountain areas. In the early days, the main form of land transport consisted of man-hauled sledges, on which both Scott and Shackleton largely relied. Amundsen first proved the worth of dog teams.

Shackleton introduced the first mechanical vehicle during his *Nimrod* expedition of 1907–9. This was an Arrol-Johnston motor car with a four-cylinder 15 hp air-cooled engine, and special steel-ribbed tyres. Scott, on his last expedition, experimented with three Wolseley motor sledges. These had full tracks and were steered by braking one track or the other. The four-cylinder air-cooled engines drove the vehicles at $3\frac{1}{2}$ mph, but on his main journey they broke down and were abandoned.

The Byrd expedition of 1933–5 carried two Snowmobiles, three Citroen cars

27. *Endurance* beset, 1915

and a Cletrac tractor. The latter could haul five tons, and was the forerunner of the heavy vehicles which now travel many thousands of miles each year over the snowfields. Byrd later experimented with a specially designed 'Snow Cruiser', with wheels 10 feet in diameter, each weighing three tons. This was a total failure as they dug themselves into even the hardest compacted snow.

After the Second World War, a number of expeditions, including the Australian and the French, began to use the wartime Weasel with considerable success. Since 1955 the variety of vehicles has increased enormously. Now there is a choice ranging from motor toboggans weighing 500 lbs, to huge 35-ton tractors capable of towing a 50-ton train of sledges. The latter are suitable only for use in open country free from crevasses. As they travel only at very low speeds, they are normally driven continuously throughout the 24 hours.

Yet even today, apart from horses, all the more primitive methods of travel have special advantages. Man-hauling is slow and limited in range, but it is cheap, useful in mountainous areas and comparatively safe. Dog-sledging

28. The British Antarctic Survey geophysical station Faraday at the Argentine Islands

29. Shackleton's Arrol-Johnston motor car

is also efficient in mountain areas where vehicles cannot penetrate, and is still probably the safest method of travel, especially among crevasses. But on open snowfields, dogs cannot compete in speed with vehicles, and they cannot carry heavy scientific equipment or the electric power to operate it. Light tractors, weighing up to three or four tons and capable of towing five to six tons, are fast in open country, and can be self-supporting in fuel for distances up to about 500 miles.

Britain and New Zealand still retain a few dog teams which do useful work around base, but since they have to be expensively fed even when not working, their role has been virtually phased out. To replace them, Skidoos, small motorised sledges ridden like a motor bike, have been developed. These 'mechanical dog teams' can tow the same load as nine dogs, and can be flown into operational areas to provide a cheaper but far less companionable form of transport for field workers.

An indispensable part of a modern expedition is its aircraft, though their use is governed by weather conditions, the terrain, and the need to provide

30. TAE *tractors in a field of sastrugi*

adequate backing in mechanics, spare parts, workshops and fuel. They have ranged from tiny two-seater planes for reconnaissance, through twin-engined Otters with a payload of one to two tons, the ski-equipped Hercules (C130) carrying 10 to 12 tons, to the United States giant-wheeled Starlifters of today. The larger planes have to be withdrawn at the end of each summer, but they are able to fly in again much earlier in the following season than an icebreaker can force a passage through the sea ice to the coast.

Small aircraft can be sufficiently protected to winter in the open. Where there are no hangars, the undercarriage is sunk into a pit facing the prevailing wind, and the ailerons, elevators and rudder removed. The wings lie horizontal to the surface, and wooden wind deflectors can be erected behind them.

Ever since 1956, Argentine and British ships have each year forced a passage through the ice-filled waters of the Weddell Sea to relieve their bases. The problem has been to know where to find the easiest passage through the pack. In 1967 the United States put a satellite, ESSA-3, into polar orbit round the Earth. During the southern summer months, this took photographs as it passed over the Antarctic every two hours. In 1968 it was replaced by ESSA-7, but this too has been superseded. The present pictures come to us from the later NOAA and NIMBUS satellites. These are transmitted to Washington where lines of latitude and longitude are superimposed on them by computer. Apart from weather and sea ice information, they provide imagery of sufficient definition for maps to be produced at a scale of 1 : 250,000. Indeed, it would be possible to provide surface elevations to an accuracy of half a metre, but so far this facility has not been used because it is too expensive to retrieve the information from the records.

Each season the series of photographs covering the British area of operations is made available to the British Antarctic Survey, where the best routes for the relief ships are assessed and the information sent to the captains. This has greatly reduced the risk of ships wasting time or becoming beset.

When purely geographical exploration was the main object, short-term expeditions lasting up to two years were normal and worthwhile. Since the emphasis has shifted to geophysical studies, it is essential that observations are continuously maintained over a period of many years. The establishment of more permanent bases produced a number of problems, some of which have not yet been solved.

The American station at McMurdo Sound is the largest complex in Antarctica. Built near Scott's first base at Hut Point on Ross Island, it resembles a sprawling frontier boom town, with wooden buildings, power lines, radio masts, and black cinder 'streets'. In summer two airstrips are used to bring in supplies and relief personnel. One is a prepared sea ice runway on which huge Starlifter jets can land until about January – after which the ice rots and breaks up.

Then air traffic moves to Williams Field, built on the ice shelf. This is shorter and can only accept the smaller ski-equipped Hercules transports. Buses leave 'town' for the airstrips every hour, and helicopters operate for 15 hours each day relieving or supplying field parties in the work areas.

The station supports a mixed population of up to 1000 during summer and about a hundred in winter. Living accommodation is comfortable, with a television set in every lounge, and five or six films are shown each evening. Ice cream is always available, and fresh meat and vegetables are flown in regularly. Everyone feeds together in 'the galley' – reputedly the largest building in Antarctica.

The station stands just below Observation Hill, on top of which a single cross commemorates Captain Scott and the four companions who died with him. Nearby Mount Erebus still gently spouts its steamy plume 12,000 feet above the 'town'.

Two thousand miles away, along the coast of the Antarctic Peninsula, there are numerous smaller British, Chilean and Argentine bases, together with one American and one Russian station, all built on rock. The Chileans operate a meteorological station, Presidente Frei, on King George Island, only a few hundred yards from the Russian, Bellingshausen. Recently they established an Air Force training base, Teniente Marsh, just a mile away. This is an air facility with a 4000-foot runway of compacted gravel and permafrost, which opened a new door to Antarctica. It has extensive transit accommodation for over 50 people, and this makes it possible to transfer incoming and outgoing passengers from the increasing number of tourist ships which now cruise along the coast of the Peninsula each season.

Five hundred miles to the east lies Signy Island, in the South Orkneys, where the British station is an incongruous mixture of styles. Beside the earlier wooden hut there now stands a newer biological laboratory put up in 1964. This two-storey, prefabricated building made of yellow plastic and fibre-glass laminate is fireproof, needs no painting, and is stressed to withstand winds of up to 120 knots.

Though these stations drift up in winter, with the return of the sun the snow melts and the buildings reappear intact above the surface. But bases such as Halley Bay, which is built on an ice shelf, have no firm foundation and pose great problems. A floating ice shelf is constantly being eroded from beneath by currents, while snowfall accumulates on top. Huts soon disappear below the surface, where tremendous pressures are exerted on them from all sides as the snow deforms and flows under its own weight. At Halley Bay a 'carpet' of expanded metal was laid down on a levelled area, and on this specially designed huts were erected. In the course of a single winter, drift had reached the eaves, and in two years the station was buried. In 10 years it was 50 feet below the surface, twisted and crushed from all sides, and had to be abandoned.

Why then do they continue to build on an ice shelf? This geophysical observatory, originally established on a short-term basis for the IGY, was found to lie not only within the maximum auroral belt, but also beneath a remarkable narrow region in space and the upper atmosphere known as the Plasmapause. The information which can be obtained at Halley Bay is so important that the Royal Society recommended to the government that the work there should be continued. Therefore, in 1959, the station was transferred to the British Antarctic Survey which has maintained it ever since.

In the summer of 1966/7 a new and stronger steel-framed base was built, but after only six years the huts were again so distorted by ice pressure that melt-water dripped through the roofs, plastic sheets had to be hung beneath the ceilings, and drainage gutters festooned the walls. Bits of string were positioned to lead dripping water into strategically placed buckets, and the laddered entrance shafts were already 30 feet below the surface.

31. Halley (IV), 1983

In order to overcome similar problems at Byrd Station, in 1962 the Americans had constructed prefabricated buildings in deep trenches covered by arched corrugated steel roofs. This was not altogether successful because heat from the huts distorted the ice walls of the trenches and the roofs became unstable, but their idea led the British to a new concept.

In 1973 a new Halley Bay was built on a fresh site inside corrugated steel tubes. Five of these were placed in line and linked by smaller passage tubes. Unfortunately, for convenience in design, the bottoms of the tubes were slightly flattened, and after a few years this showed up as the weak point as once more pressure began to distort the structures.

In addition, because of the constant seaward movement of the ice shelf itself, the base was becoming exposed to the danger of breaking away in a calving iceberg. Indeed, in 1977 large portions of the headlands calved off and drifted out to sea. Suddenly Halley Bay lost its 'bay' and the station was renamed Halley. Four years later the original IGY huts began to appear in the face of the ice cliff.

32. *Part of Little America* V *floating out to sea in an iceberg*

By 1983 Halley was again deeply buried and becoming a fire hazard. It was time for yet another rebuild. Halley (IV) was erected seven miles in from the ice edge – and to yet another design. Two-storey blocks were constructed inside completely circular wooden tubes. The planning phase had included computer simulation of stresses and deformation, with rigorous tests being made on the panels for structural strength and moisture penetration. If this design succeeds the base can be used until it becomes too deeply buried under the ever-accumulating snow. To the last problem there is as yet no answer.

But to men living in buried buildings, and in a waterless land, fire is perhaps the greatest hazard of all. Over the years a number of disastrous incidents, resulting in loss of life, have ensured that stringent safety precautions are enforced at the bases. Huts are built with escape exits, and one man (usually the meteorological observer) always remains awake at night to watch over generators and fires. Emergency stocks of food, fuel and clothing are kept in a separate building some distance away from main living quarters. Fire drill is practised regularly, and fire-fighting appliances are regularly checked.

It is often thought that with tractors, aircraft, radio and other modern equipment, polar exploration today is without the hazards which faced the early pioneers. To some extent this is true. We now know much more about sledging diets, vitamins, clothing and safer techniques of travel. But modern methods have produced a different set of problems, and brought their own dangers.

At the beginning of this century it was necessary to lay a series of depots before a long journey could be attempted. Today tractor parties can set out relying on aircraft to bring in their supplies. But with tractors weighing up to 35 tons, routes have to be most carefully selected. The problem of crossing crevassed zones is far more difficult and dangerous, for vehicles fall into bridged cracks and chasms which dog teams would cross without even knowing they existed.

In a land where 'whiteout' merges the sky with the ground, where winds blow at 150 mph and low drift constantly obscures the surface, it takes courage to fly. Every time an aircraft takes off it is at risk, for there are few reliable weather forecasts and few navigational aids. Many planes and helicopters have crashed, and numerous lives have been lost.

Radio too has its disadvantages, for there is a tendency to rely too much on good communications. During magnetic storms radio can fail for days at a time, preventing a call for assistance being heard. Men who were at one moment flying in comfort, can quickly find themselves alone on the ground with little hope of telling their base where they have landed. For this reason all planes carry rations and survival equipment, and many crews have had to make use of them.

In spite of modern methods and improved equipment, men who work in Antarctica still need toughness and self reliance. They have to know the old techniques, and in time of trouble be ready to use them. Their work is, in fact, increasingly complicated by the new equipment which, at first sight, would seem to have removed difficulties and risks.

14
International Laboratory

With the advent of satellites there are no new features to be discovered in Antarctica, for their all-seeing eyes have revealed every mountain, cape and island. But even before the arrival of this sophisticated tool geographical discovery had largely given way to scientific investigation. In nearly all fields of study the first requirement is a map of the area. Aerial photography and satellite imagery now provide relatively easy methods of getting the basic outlines. However, the pictures obtained by either method cannot be turned into maps without knowing the precise position of some of the features – and this can be established only by men on the ground.

Surveyors must climb up to high positions, from where they can measure angles and distances to build up a geometrical network of triangles, to which all the other features in the photographs can be related. Theodolites are used to measure horizontal angles and the vertical angles which give height. But today tellurometers, which employ radio waves to measure the distance between two points with extreme accuracy, are also widely used.

Since a significant portion of the world's water is held in cold storage in Antarctica, glaciology is an important study. Precipitation, which would fall as rain in temperate climates, here drifts down in swirling clouds of snowflakes. In the low temperatures they do not melt, but form an ever-thickening carpet which gradually changes its consistency. Under their own weight, and scoured by the winds, the delicate snow crystals change into coarse granules. As one digs deeper into the surface, the soft texture gives way to something more like sand, and then to a consolidated icy mass. At depths of 300 feet or more it has attained the consistency of true ice.

When sufficient ice is piled up on a steep slope, it deforms and begins to 'flow' under its own weight. Thus glaciers fill the valleys, and the great ice sheet which covers Antarctica is itself very slowly sliding outwards towards the oceans. Every year, huge masses break off from the edge to form thousands of icebergs, which finally melt in the sea.

Glaciologists study the ice to find out how it affects the rest of the world – How thick is it? Is it increasing or getting less? What are the temperatures within it? What lies under it? – In 1968 the Americans at Byrd drilled a hole through 7000 feet of ice to the rock below. This produced a continuous core four and a half inches in diameter. In the upper sections, layers showed each separate year's snowfall, just as the rings found in tree trunks show the annual growth. Much was learnt from this, not only about variations in the world's climate thousands of years ago, but also how much the atmosphere was contaminated by the industrial revolution, and even about the rate at which cosmic dust falls on the Earth from outer space. When the ice-corer reached the bottom, water rose up into the bore-hole. This proved a theory that at such depths the heat coming from the interior of the Earth raises the temperature enough for the ice to melt under its own enormous weight. It could, therefore, slide catastrophically.

British scientists at the Scott Polar Research Institute, Cambridge, have invented a radar which can be fitted in an aircraft to make continuous photographic records of ice thickness wherever the plane may fly. Signals are beamed downwards from an antenna under the plane, and echoes come back both from the ice surface and the bedrock below. The equipment not only measures the depth of ice cover, but also reveals the mountains, valleys and plains which lie underneath. In the course of an hour's flight more data can thus be brought back than could be obtained from many seasons of seismic sounding on the ground.

Over many thousands of years, there have been great changes in the extent and thickness of the ice sheet. If this is now decreasing, the Earth will receive more heat from the sun's radiation and the cooling of the atmosphere will be less. (At present most of the radiation falling on snow is reflected by the white surface.) This in turn will affect air circulation, and could alter the present weather systems everywhere.

All continents are made of lighter rock than the main mass of the world. They can be thought of as 'floating', rather like a cork on water. An appreciable reduction of the ice cover would reduce the weight resting on the continent, and this would allow the land to rise. Such a rising would be very slow – perhaps only one foot in a hundred years. But even at that rate beaches which now lie around the coast would be 10 feet above sea level in a thousand years' time. A number of raised beaches, from 10 to 300 feet above present sea level, have already been found in the Antarctic, so we know the ice cover was once much greater than it is today.

Geologists have discovered that the oldest Antarctic rocks were formed 4000 million years ago. Many different types have been evolved through the ages, among which are sandstones or limestones which contain fossils. These beautifully preserved impressions of leaves, flowers, insect wings and so on, show that about 15 million years ago the climate was temperate, and that 50 million years ago tropical plants flourished. For a long time it was believed that the climate of Antarctica had changed, but now nearly all geologists accept the theory of 'continental drift'.

They reason that the existence of tropical plants in the ancient rocks proves

33. Australian surveyors using a tellurometer

that the continent itself has moved and drifted to its present position. This would explain why the same fossil plants have been found in Australia, South Africa, Madagascar, southern India and Antarctica. It is becoming generally accepted that at one time these lands were all joined together, forming a great super-continent which geologists call Gondwana. It later broke up into the smaller landmasses we know today, and Antarctica 'floated' into a frigid zone which killed the flora.

Magnetic observations have provided further evidence for the drift theory. Many of the rocks were formed from hot molten material rising from within the Earth, and as it cooled and crystallized, the iron-rich crystals arranged themselves north/south in the Earth's magnetic field as it was at the time. Specimens collected today give evidence of the direction of magnetism which existed millions of years ago. This 'fossil magnetism' indicates where the continent was in relation to the Magnetic Pole at the time the rocks were formed. These measurements, too, confirm that Antarctica has drifted into its present position through many millions of years.

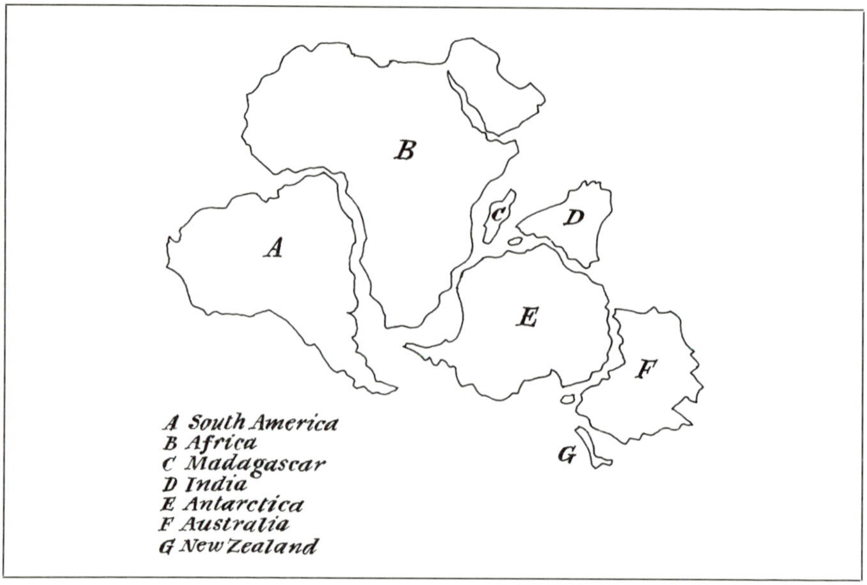

Map 7. Gondwana

Geologists are also exploring the rocks for minerals, and examining the way in which the mountains have been built up. The great Andean mountain chain in Chile extends eastwards in a huge submarine ridge, the Scotia Ridge, which loops southwards and westwards to join the continental mainland through the Antarctic Peninsula. Not only do we find similar rocks and fossils in South America and Antarctica, but clearly it was the same mountain-building forces which affected both continents.

Curiously, although rich mineral deposits are found in South America, none have so far been discovered in the Antarctic. Enormous coalfields exist, but it is impossible to mine or transport the coal economically. Almost certainly there are other valuable minerals, but at present there is little chance of discovering them beneath the great ice sheet.

Geophysical studies concentrate especially on the ionosphere, a layer about 100 miles deep of ionized gas which envelopes the Earth. It begins some 60 miles above the world, and it is this layer which reflects radio waves transmitted from the ground, and makes long-distance communication possible. When particles are emitted from the sun they cause ionospheric and magnetic storms. These tear 'holes' in the envelope so that instead of being reflected back, radio waves can escape through the holes into space, causing radio blackouts.

The lines of magnetic force encircle the globe from the Arctic to the Antarctic, and direct the particles coming from the sun towards the Magnetic Poles. It is these particles, together with solar X-rays, which produce the wonderful curtains of aurorae which appear in the polar skies during the dark winter months. Studies of the interaction between the atmosphere, the solar particles, and the Earth's magnetic field are particularly effective in the polar regions, particularly the Antarctic.

Halley lies in exactly the right position to study the interaction of the ionosphere and the magnetosphere, and in 1981 the British Antarctic Survey established an Advanced Ionospheric Sounder (AIS) there. This is one of only six so far built by the National Oceanic and Atmospheric Administration (NOAA) in the United States. It is a highly sophisticated instrument, with an internal computer which can interpret and log incoming data on site. Previously this all had to be brought back and computed at home. It has made possible a variety of highly complex studies, and the researcher can modify his experiment without delay and on the spot.

Furthermore, the results can be transmitted through a satellite radio link direct to Cambridge Headquarters. It may not be long before a worker will be able to carry out his experiments in Antarctica from his desk in England – which will be very efficient, but perhaps not half such fun for the adventurous scientist longing to see the world.

The animals and primitive plants found around the continent are especially interesting to biologists, because they all have to survive under extreme conditions, and special adaptations can be observed. As the number of different species is small and the communities are simple, it is relatively easy to discover how they live and react one with another. This knowledge can then be applied to the much more complicated communities in temperate and tropical regions.

On land, and in the freshwater lakes which form in summer, conditions are very hard for the smaller forms of life. During winter, most of them are completely frozen and inert, and the mechanism which enables them to survive is not yet understood. The sea temperature is very constant and always near to freezing point. Along the coast, conditions are governed by the sea ice which scrubs the rocks and churns up the shallows. Only in crevices in the rocks or in deeper water can growth proceed naturally.

Life on the sea bottom is studied at the British base on Signy Island. Skin divers work down to depths of 100 feet, but because of the cold, they can remain down for only about twenty minutes at a time. Coming out of the water is often a severe experience, for the air temperature is usually much lower than it is under the ice. If there is a wind blowing as well, a man in a wet suit can quickly freeze up, so a tent is normally pitched at the water's edge, with a Primus stove kept burning inside, and here a diver can immediately change into dry clothes.

Unlike men, whales and seals can dive to very great depths without getting 'the bends', a condition caused by atmospheric nitrogen being dissolved in the blood. It is possible that they empty their lungs before going down, so that no nitrogen is available, and they probably survive on oxygen absorbed by the blood corpuscles. Studies are being made to investigate this.

Penguins are also the subject of much interest. For six years a United States research team studied the Emperors and Adélies at Cape Crozier, first visited by Wilson, Bowers and Cherry-Garrard during Scott's last expedition. Russian scientists have been doing similar work at Mirny, trying to find out more about the 'homing' mechanism of these strange birds. One experiment entailed flying some penguins from both bases to the South Pole, where they were released. After staring at the sun for a while, the birds immediately set off for the sea, each group plodding along in the direction of its own colony. As soon as the sky became overcast they wandered about aimlessly. Clearly they were using the sun for navigation, correcting their course to allow for its daily circuit round the polar sky. So far no one has discovered how this 'inner clock' works.

Another mystery is how do parents and chicks recognise each other in a colony of, say, 200,000 penguins? To help in solving this, tiny transmitters which trace their movements have been attached to marked birds. They have also been placed inside eggs where they can record temperature changes during incubation.

In the Ross Dependency, under the towering mountains of the Royal Society Range, lie a series of 'dry valleys'. One of these ice-free areas was first seen by Scott during his *Discovery* expedition, but the reason why the ice has retreated is not yet certain. Clearly the glaciers which once occupied the valleys have disappeared because the supply of ice was insufficient to sustain them. This implies reduced snow precipitation and reduction of the ice sheet, which was then adequately drained by adjacent valley glaciers – leaving no ice to be channelled into the now dry valleys.

The primitive soils of these valleys were studied in the interests of the American Space Programme. The purpose was to help in the design of automated systems for recognising life in the cold arid conditions on the Moon or on Mars. Thus in this and other ways, Antarctica has been a testing ground for physicists, biologists and medical doctors responsible for the work of United States astronauts.

34 and 35. Elephant seals, Macquarie Island; and, below, Weddell seal pup

EPILOGUE

15
Whither Antarctica?

We have traced the broad history of Antarctic exploration and seen how the early urge to geographical discovery gradually gave place to scientific investigation. Indeed, increasingly it was found that the Antarctic regions are able to provide experimental fields, or fields of study in very many sciences which can provide answers unobtainable in other parts of the world – even the Arctic. Today budding scientists can look forward to taking part in really exciting advances in Antarctica, whatever their subject may be. But apart from occasional theoretical inspiration, science tends to progress by patient continuous observation and experiment.

It follows that one can rarely report spectacular discoveries at any particular stage. Nevertheless, the excitement of participating in on-going sequences of discovery has been, and remains, exceptionally rewarding in a region which is still relatively unknown.

Antarctic science has reached a high degree of sophistication, and now the world at large is beginning to ask where the material profits may be. There lies the boundary between pure science and the advent of technologies based on our existing knowledge of resources. Although fish and 'krill' are already being exploited commercially, it is really the expectation of minerals and oil that excites the natural cupidity of nations. Yet no exploitable mineral resources have so far been found, and it is not even known that oil actually exists in the few geologically suitable areas. No one would deny that such resources *may* be there, but the general expectancy seems to be rooted more in reiterated press reports that Antarctica is a 'rich storehouse of minerals' than in scientific knowledge.

Goaded by such ill-informed statements, an increasing number of amazingly disparate countries has been hastening to accede to the Antarctic Treaty. (Brazil, Bulgaria, Czechoslovakia, Denmark, Federal German Republic, German Democratic Republic, Italy, Netherlands, Peru, Poland, Romania, Spain, Uruguay and, most recently, China and India.) No one wants to miss out on the expected bonanza. It has even been suggested that the original Treaty Powers are merely an exclusive club with only their own interests at heart, and that Antarctica should now be handed over to the United Nations.

This would scarcely please the nations with territorial claims, nor even those who have for many years, and at considerable expense, put enormous effort into scientific investigations. Furthermore, the control of operations in such a region, where the natural conditions demand long years of experience in order to be able to judge those things which can or cannot be done, requires highly specialised knowledge. The techniques of just living and performing the simplest tasks have to be learnt, let alone the problems of mounting major operations in an attempt to extract economically any potential wealth.

Under the umbrella of the Treaty it has often been difficult enough to persuade twelve countries to agree on sound practical conservation measures. The mind boggles at the thought of politicians from 150 countries at the United Nations, inexperienced in what the problems really are, attempting to dictate the future of the continent.

If it was left as a natural wilderness and a laboratory for pure science, there would be no greater problems than those which have been argued and resolved by the mechanism of the Treaty. But as it seems most unlikely that this will be an acceptable final solution, it would seem perhaps both sensible and prudent to leave commercial exploitation to the nations with experience who have the necessary advanced technology. By international agreement, it would then be quite possible to siphon off a portion of the profits for the benefit of needy Third World countries not directly involved.

Today another factor has been added to the general political rumblings and undercurrents, for a strong conservation lobby is making its voice heard. As things stand Antarctica is better controlled and protected by conservation measures than any other region in the world. This has been achieved through the various regulations established under the Treaty, and is a powerful reason why interested nations should accede to it, for by doing so they submit their nationals to all the controls which have been worked out.

Conservationists would rightly protest vigorously at any 'do-it-yourself' opportunist country which attempted to go its own way to the detriment of the environment. In 1977 the Treaty Powers agreed that they would not undertake any commercial exploration or exploitation anywhere on the continent before the adoption of a sensible minerals regime. This is now under serious discussion, and it would indeed be tragic to see such a measure destroyed by a babel of dissident voices.

For all the forebodings there is one surprising and valuable resource available which could be used without any kind of environmental damage. For a number of years studies have been made regarding the use of icebergs as a source of freshwater for arid regions. Calculations indicate that the cost would be less than it is for the desalination of sea water. All that is lacking is the technology to do it.

How are icebergs to be harnessed and towed? How should they be handled if they fragment, tilt or capsize in rough seas during the tow? How close can they be brought to land when their draft is as much as 800 feet or more? How is the freshwater to be confined and transported ashore? How destructive will the sudden introduction of such masses of cold water be to tropical marine life? These and associated questions have yet to be answered, but the concept is an exciting one, and will undoubtedly one day prove to be a blessing to many hot dry countries.

The sub-Antarctic island of South Georgia is already the centre of a wonderfully rewarding conservation success story. The near extermination of the fur seals during the nineteenth century left a few isolated groups in the region of the Scotia Sea. One of these tiny populations of some seventy animals was reported on Bird Island (off South Georgia) in 1935. Protected by Falkland Islands law which also applied to South Georgia as a dependency, the taking of fur seals for any reason was totally prohibited – since when they have successfully multipled until in 1983 they were estimated to number 900,000 on and around the main island. Some have migrated to their old haunts in the South Sandwich and South Shetland Islands where the numbers are also steadily increasing. So Man *can* repair the damage he has inflicted in the past if there is the will to do so.

Another factor which may perhaps have some deleterious impact on the fragile ecological balance of the continent unless it can be properly controlled is tourism. Already several commercial companies promote a number of cruises each season along the coast of the Antarctic Peninsula. At present this is a very expensive holiday available only for the rich, and therefore the numbers are relatively small. Those put ashore to visit bases or penguin colonies are always under strict and experienced control, both for their own personal safety and also to ensure that no damage is done to nesting sites or to the sparse vegetation. Up to now tourists have been made very much aware of the ground rules, and have been remarkably conscientious in their cooperation and behaviour.

Yet looking to the future, it is possible to envisage the erection of hotels ashore – even sports centres – which would draw numbers of eager but totally unaware visitors. These could almost certainly be sited within easy access of penguin rookeries, which would hardly be expected to survive constant visitations. Add to this all the inevitable problems of litter and the need to dispose of bulk waste, and the damage to the local environment could become severe – as it has in so many other beautiful parts of the world.

Should such a threat become a reality it will be incumbent upon the Antarctic community of nations to establish, and somehow to enforce rigorous ground rules of behaviour – however unwelcome these might be to the operating companies. Today mining, drilling for oil and mass tourism are only potential threats in the distant future. Yet it would be wise to remain alert to the damaging possibilities, and to be prepared to fight for the preservation of the last clean continent, as yet hardly sullied by Man.

Antarctica is one of the power houses of the world's weather systems. Its ice contains a continuous record of past climates and both natural and man-made pollutants. It has been found to hold the key to many scientific problems affecting the whole Earth. We must surely hope that territorial claims and political rivalries can be resolved, so that unfettered freedom to continue such work in an untainted environment will continue to bring knowledge beneficial to all mankind.

36. The new Wilkes Station, built on stilts to discourage drift accumulation

Chronological list of the main Antarctic expeditions since the first landings on the continent, and of books written about them in English.

1897–9	**Belgian Antarctic Expedition: A. de Gerlache** COOK, F. A. *Through the first Antarctic night.* Heinemann, London, 1900.
1898–1900	**British Antarctic Expedition: C. E. Borchgrevink** BORCHGREVINK, C. E. *First on the Antarctic continent.* Newnes, London, 1901.
1901–3	**Swedish South Polar Expedition: O. Nordenskjold** NORDENSKJOLD, O. *and* J. G. ANDERSSON. *Antarctica or two years amongst the ice of the South Pole.* Hurst & Blackett, London, 1905.
1901–4	**British National Antarctic Expedition: R. F. Scott** SCOTT, R. F. *Voyage of the 'Discovery'*, 2 volumes. Smith Elder, London, 1905. WILSON, E. A. *Diary of the 'Discovery' expedition to the Antarctic regions 1901–1904.* ed. A. Savours. Blandford, London, 1966.
1902–4	**Scottish National Antarctic Expedition: W. S. Bruce** RUDMOSE BROWN, R. N., R. C. MOSSMAN *and* J. H. HARVEY PIRIE. *The voyage of the 'Scotia'.* Blackwood, Edinburgh, 1906.
1907–9	**British Antarctic Expedition: E. H. Shackleton** SHACKLETON, E. H. *The heart of the Antarctic*, 2 volumes. Heinemann, London, 1909.
1908–10	**French Antarctic Expedition: J. B. Charcot** CHARCOT, J. B. *The voyage of the 'Why Not' in the Antarctic.* Hodder & Stoughton, London, 1911.
1910–12	**Norwegian Antarctic Expedition: R. Amundsen** AMUNDSEN, R. *The South Pole*, 2 volumes. Murray, London, 1912.
1910–13	**British National Antarctic Expedition: R. F. Scott** ARMITAGE, A. B. *Two years in the Antarctic.* Arnold, London, 1905. CHERRY-GARRARD, A. *The worst journey in the world.* Chatto & Windus, London, 1965. EVANS, R. J. R. *South with Scott.* Collins, London, 1921. PRIESTLEY, R. E. *Antarctic adventure.* Unwin, London, 1914. SCOTT, R. F. *Scott's last expedition; the personal journals of R. F. Scott* CVO RN *on his journey to the South Pole.* Folio Society, London, 1964.
1911–14	**Australasian Antarctic Expedition: D. Mawson** HURLEY, F. *Argonauts of the South.* Putnam, New York, 1925. LASERON, C. F. *South with Mawson.* Angus & Robertson, Sydney, 1947. MAWSON, D. *The home of the blizzard*, 2 volumes. Heinemann, London, 1915.
1914–16	**Imperial Trans-Antarctic Expedition: Sir Ernest Shackleton** LANCING, A. *Endurance.* Hodder & Stoughton, London, 1959. SHACKLETON, SIR ERNEST, *South.* Heinemann, London, 1919. WORSLEY, F. A. *Endurance: an epic of polar adventure.* Geoffrey Bless, London, 1931.

1914–17 **Shackleton's Ross Sea Party: A. Mackintosh**
RICHARDS, R. W. *The Ross Sea Shore Party 1914–17*. Scott Polar Research Institute, Cambridge, 1962.

1928–30 **United States Antarctic Expedition: R. E. Byrd**
BYRD, R. E. *Little America*. Putnam, London, 1931.

1933–5 **United States Antarctic Expedition: R. E. Byrd**
BYRD, R. E. *Alone*. Putnam, London, 1958.

1934–7 **British Graham Land Expedition: J. Rymill**
RYMILL, J. *Southern lights*. Chatto & Windus, London, 1938.

1943 **Falkland Island Dependencies Survey – British Antarctic Survey**
ANDERSON, E. *Expedition south*. Evans Bros, London, 1957.
FUCHS, SIR VIVIAN. *of Ice and men*. Anthony Nelson, Oswestry. Shropshire, 1982.
HERBERT, W. *A world of men*. Eyre & Spottiswoode, London, 1968.
JAMES, D. *That frozen land*. Falcon Press, London, 1949.
WALTON, E. W. K. *Two years in the Antarctic*. Lutterworth, London, 1955.

1947 **Australian National Antarctic Research Expedition**
BROWN, P. L. *Twelve came back*. Hale, London, 1957.
DOVERS, R. *Huskies*. Bell, London, 1957.
SCHOLES, A. *Fourteen men*. Allen & Unwin, London, 1951.

1947–8 **American Antarctic Expedition: F. Ronne**
DARLINGTON, MRS J. *My Antarctic honeymoon*. Muller, London, 1957.
RONNE, F. *Antarctic conquest*. Putnam, New York, 1949.

1949–51 **Norwegian-British-Swedish Expedition: J. Giaever**
GIAEVER, J. *The white desert*. Chatto & Windus, London, 1954.
SCHOLES, A. *Fourteen men*. Allen & Unwin, London, 1951.

1955–8 **Commonwealth Trans-Antarctic Expedition: V. E. Fuchs**
FUCHS, SIR VIVIAN *and* SIR EDMUND HILLARY. *The Crossing of Antarctica*. Cassells, London, 1958.
FUCHS, SIR VIVIAN. *Antarctic adventure* (the story of the expedition written for young people). Cassells, London, 1959.
HELM, A. S. *and* J. H. MILLER. *Antarctica*. Government Printer, Wellington, 1964.

Further background readimg

PRIESTLEY, SIR RAYMOND, R. J. ADIE, G. DE Q. ROBIN, ed. *Antarctic research*. Butterworth, London, 1964.
HATHERTON, TREVOR, ed. *Antarctica*. Methuen, London, 1965.
KING, H. G. R. *Introducing the Antarctic*. Blandford, London, 1969.
QUIGG, PHILIP W. *A Pole Apart: the Emerging Issue of Antarctica*. A Twentieth Century Fund Report. McGraw-Hill, New York, 1983.

INDEX

Figures in bold type refer to page number of illustrations